To Cynthia,
With grateful thanks for
all your love and support
during the difficult years.
Much love,
Ros

Sailing in Deep Waters

"To Him who loves us and released us from our sins
by His blood…. to Him be the glory and the dominion
forever and ever."

To a great couple whose kindness has made my life much easier – Yvonne who came round three times a week when Ellen was a baby to relieve me of housework chores and support me with her friendship, and Martin whose patience and kindness helped me through the hardest days of my life.

Introduction

In March of last year I started keeping a blog http://rosbunneywriting.wordpress.com. I had no idea at the time what an eventful period lay ahead of me. I also had no idea that people would take an interest in my blog. At first friends kindly followed it, and then people who didn't know me began to take an interest. One post in particular (No.5) has brought people to my blog via a search engine almost every day since I posted it. And when I began chronicling my experience of bereavement, that seemed to touch a chord with many people, unsurprisingly I suppose, as death touches all of us at some time in our lives.

Now I have gathered these posts together into this book, and seeing them one after the other on the page like this, I realise that many of them deal with the troubles and difficulties we experience in life. I think this is inevitable when I am just emerging from a troubled period! Perhaps my future posts will be more to do with the joy and wonder of this amazing life God has given us.

I hope, though, that the one thing that comes across is that the faithfulness, love and compassion of God are at their brightest when life is at its darkest. If readers only take one thing from this book I hope it is that Jesus is beautiful, faithful, wonderful and worthy of all our worship. If you are struggling with life's difficulties yourself, I pray that these writings will encourage you to set aside some time every day just to stop, be alone, sit in silence and stillness, and allow Him to speak to your heart whatever He wants to say to you. If someone grows into a deeper relationship of intimacy with Jesus through reading any of what I have written, the writing will have been well worthwhile.

The cover picture is a photograph I took a few years ago of Collioure in the South of France, where the church tower doubles as a lighthouse. I love the idea of a building which both hosts the worship of God and keeps sailors away from danger. I hope that some of what I've written has thrown light on the safe channels in which you can make your voyage. I have sailed through some deep waters in the past few years, but the shallows are not a safe place – the lighthouse warns of submerged rocks and sandbanks on which a vessel could be wrecked. As you sail your own journey through the storms and calms of life, may the light of God's word and the fellowship of His people keep you in safe waters with your compass needle pointing towards harbour.

1. The Eternal God

I was talking with friends tonight about what it means for God to be eternal. It sounds like a dry and dusty doctrine, something we are supposed to believe about God, but which at first glance doesn't appear to have much to do with our lives. I have gradually come to have a very different view of it.

If God stands outside of time, He doesn't have the same linear view of it that we have. That sounds like stating the obvious, but it's only recently that I've started to appreciate what that actually means, for me, in practical terms. From where I stand now, on 3rd March 2012, aged 53 and three-quarters, the present moment is this one now where I am sitting in my living room with my laptop, typing this. Behind me lies the past, some of it now completely lost to me in obscurity, some dimly or perhaps inaccurately remembered, some as vivid in my recollection now as the moment when it happened. Before me stretches the future, and although I am shaping and creating it by the decisions I take and the words I speak and write now, still I have only an imprecise sense of what will happen. There are no doubt many events I haven't anticipated, and though I know what dreams I hope to realise, I can't see exactly how they will become reality.

But for God it isn't like that. He doesn't have our linear view of time, although in the person of Jesus He subjected Himself to it, and He fully understands it from our point of view. God stands outside of our space-time dimensions, and therefore every single location in space and every single moment in time is continually present to Him.

Understanding this had a very profound effect on me. I have always believed that God can heal me of things that have damaged me in the past. But this was merely a theoretical belief, and one that gave me great difficulty when I tried to visualise it. Recalling a particularly traumatic incident that occurred when I was 13, someone once advised me to think back to those events and see Jesus present with me. It simply didn't work. If He was present, why didn't He stop it happening? God is supposed to be my Father. If a human Father, with power to intervene, witnessed that happening to His daughter, and did nothing to stop it, we would call it child abuse.

But understanding the eternity of God changed my whole perspective on this. If every single moment of time is eternally present to God, then He is still right there when that incident happened. To me it is something in my past that left its mark on me. But it is still present to God right here and now (of course if God is outside space and time, then "here" and "now" are concessions to our limited understanding. Then again, the God who is outside time and space chooses to step into time and space, not just at some particular point in history, but constantly, again and again, so these two words are not meaningless). If God is currently present at that moment in my history, then He can change it right now. The past is not set in stone. He is there, now, as it happens, and He is healing the damage it did to me. Once I saw this I understood how He really can heal the wounds of the past by being there now and changing their effect on me, and I truly did experience healing and freedom from the effects of what had happened.

Of course the flip side of this is that He is in my future, too, right at this very moment. Dreams I am dreaming, prayers whose answers I am waiting for, they are all happening right now where He is. If I can learn to align myself with Him, I can be there too, and I can pull my future into the present. I'm still working on this! One day I know I will see my daughter get up out of her wheelchair and walk. But this new perspective means I don't simply have to wait passively hoping it will someday happen. God is right there in her future at this very moment, making it happen. The more I align myself with Him, the closer I come to pulling that event into the present. How exciting, to be a co-creator with Him in this way.

2. "When Israel was a child I loved him... it is I who taught Ephraim to walk; I took them in my arms" (Hosea 11)

I was recently watching a father with his young son. The fascinating thing about the scene was that this little boy was adopted, not because the parents had decided to adopt another child, but because the social workers had come to a couple who had thought their family was complete, and asked them to adopt another child in desperate need of a loving home, and moved by love, they had opened their hearts to him and made him a part of their family.

The father was sitting on the floor teaching his son to walk. He stood him up against the sofa and then sat so that when they both extended their arms fully, he was about an inch out of reach. Tentatively the little boy leaned forward until he could just about touch his daddy's fingertips, and then dared to put one foot forward. Holding onto his daddy's hands, he continued to take faltering steps until finally he was near enough to collapse into his father's arms.

Over and over again they repeated the process, and what struck me most of all, even more than the boy's growing confidence, was the look of radiant delight on the father's face with every successful step that his little boy took. His joy was infectious and soon his little son began to feel real pride in his achievement, as he saw how proud his daddy was of him.

Eventually the lad became tired. He tried to take the next step, but he was just too weary to go on; his little knees buckled beneath him and he sank to the floor. Without a moment's hesitation his father scooped him up in his arms, held him close to his heart and smothered him with kisses. Before long the two of them were giggling together.

For me it was the most beautiful picture of God's fatherhood. Paul tells us in Romans 8 that we have received a spirit of adoption as sons by which we cry out, "Abba! Father!" The Spirit Himself testifies with our spirit that we are children of God. But I have often looked at other Christians and compared myself unfavourably with them. Their walk with God is so much more consistent than mine, so much more confident and faith-filled than mine, and I've had this image of God tolerating me because He has to, while I wear His patience thin.

But watching this scene of a father with his adopted son it brought home to me that God delights in every step I take, however faltering. If I sometimes miss my step, or lack confidence, or doubt whether His arms are really there to catch me, it doesn't make a scrap of difference to the joy and excitement with which He watches and encourages my feeblest attempts. And when I fail totally to take the steps I should, and fall flat on my face, far from condemning me, He scoops me up in His arms, holds me close to His heart and showers me with love.

For a long time I've called God my Father without really believing the implications of it. But seeing how much a human father can pour healing love on his adopted son recalled to mind for me Jesus' words: "If you sinful people know how to give good gifts to your children, how much more will your heavenly Father give good gifts to those who ask him." If the love and delight a human father takes in his child is so great and has such profound effects, how immense and real and life-changing is God's love!

3. Unless you become like a little child…

1 Samuel 30 : "Then it happened when David and his men came to Ziklag on the third day, that the Amalekites had made a raid on the Negev and on Ziklag, and had overthrown Ziklag and burned it with fire; and they took captive the women and all who were in it, both small and great, without killing anyone, and carried them off and went their way. When David and his men came to the city, behold, it was burned with fire, and their wives and their sons and their daughters had been taken captive. Then David and the people who were with him lifted their voices and wept until there was no strength in them to weep. Now David's two wives had been taken captive, Ahinoam the Jezreelitess and Abigail the widow of Nabal the Carmelite. Moreover David was greatly distressed because the people spoke of stoning him, for all the people were embittered, each one because of his sons and his daughters. But David strengthened himself in the LORD his God. Then David said to Abiathar the priest, the son of Ahimelech, "Please bring me the ephod." So Abiathar brought the ephod to David. David inquired of the LORD, saying, "Shall I pursue this band? Shall I overtake them?" And He said to him, "Pursue, for you will surely overtake them, and you will surely rescue all.".... So David recovered all that the Amalekites had taken, and rescued his two wives. But nothing of theirs was missing, whether small or great, sons or daughters, spoil or anything that they had taken for themselves; David brought it all back."

Imagine being one of David's children. Your father has gone out to fight, and the Amalekites have seized the opportunity to make a raid on his camp, and his wives and children – including you – have been taken captive, and all your possessions stolen. You sit there, not knowing what is going on. You don't know where your father is. You don't know if he's even aware you've been captured, but there's no reason to suppose he knows. You're cold, tired, hungry, frightened, disorientated. You have no idea what's going to happen to you.

What you don't know is what's going on back at the camp. Your father has arrived back and discovered what's happened. He is so distraught that he cries aloud until he is exhausted by emotion and has no strength left to weep – that's how much he cares about you. Everyone else is blaming him for what's happened, which greatly increases his distress. But he turns to God and recovers his strength in Him. Then he seeks God's counsel as to how to proceed, and God tells him how to pursue the enemy and rescue everyone.

But chained up in the enemy camp, you have no idea of all this. You sit there as hour after hour ticks by. You see no change in your situation. You have no way of knowing what the outcome will be, except that based on past experience you have every reason to expect that the Amalekites will kill their captives.

Meantime, your captors are eating, drinking and dancing – celebrating the trauma they've inflicted on you. All you can do is sit there in despair and fear, listening to the sound of their celebrations.

Suddenly you begin to hear a different sound, dimly in the distance at first, but rapidly growing nearer and clearer. It's the roar and thunder of an advancing army. And as they arrive where you are, one voice is distinctly heard above the tumult, giving orders to the army. It's your father's voice! He knows what's happened to you, he knows where you are, and he's come to rescue you. As night falls, and for the rest of the night, the sounds you hear are the sounds of battle, the sounds of your enemy being overpowered and slaughtered, the sounds of your freedom being won!

There's nothing you can contribute to this process. You're tied up with the other captives, and the only possible role for you is to sit passively while your father deals with the enemy and secures your freedom. But even though you are still cold, tired, hungry, disorientated, bound, you're no longer frightened. Because your dad is on the case, and he always wins. As day breaks, your dad and his victorious army appear among you, cutting bonds and setting prisoners free. You run into your father's arms and he says, "I missed you so much! You wouldn't believe how much I cried! But it's all right now – I've got you."

What can I learn from this? In the darkness of captivity, when it seems the enemy of my soul has overwhelmed me, as I wrestle futilely with a powerful foe, battering my puny fists ineffectually against his armour, all that happens is that I exhaust myself, and am no nearer to winning my freedom. In the fear and disorientation I can't see what my Father is doing behind the scenes, and sometimes I may wonder if He even cares.

The reality is that He is breaking His heart over my plight – lifting up His voice and weeping until He has no tears left to cry. And even as He does so He is being unfairly blamed and accused for all the world's wrongs. Then He gathers up all His divine strength and sets out to overpower the enemy.

David saw this parallel between how he as a warrior-father had acted and how God would act on his behalf. That's why he wrote, "My enemy will say, 'I have overcome him' and my adversaries will rejoice when I am shaken. But I have trusted in your lovingkindness; my heart shall rejoice in Your salvation." (Psalm 13.4-5) He knew that what he, as a warrior-father, did to rescue his family, God, as his Warrior-Father, would do no less.

So even now, as the sound of my enemy's gloating and rejoicing rings in my ears, my role is to be that of a little child, and do – nothing. There's nothing effective I can do! My only role right now is to be passive and to wait and trust while my Father overpowers the enemy, wins the victory and secures my freedom. Any action on my part is futile and a waste of energy.

And yet this perspective transforms my captivity. The cold, the dark, the hunger, the tiredness, the disorientation remain as real, as present and as unchanged as ever. And yet... and yet.

My Father, moved to the very core of His being by my situation, is riding out to my rescue. And so the fear and hopelessness evaporate, and instead of waiting for the enemy to finish the job and execute the prisoner, I'm waiting in quiet anticipation for the victory to be completed. And there's absolutely nothing I can contribute to that process, except, as a child, to wait patiently and trustingly for my Father to accomplish the task, joyful in the knowledge that He never fails, and it's only a matter of time – His time, in His purposes.

"Do not rejoice over me, O my enemy. Though I fall I will rise; though I dwell in darkness, the Lord is a light for me." (Micah 7.8)

4.   Purim

As I write this, it is the feast of Purim in the Jewish calendar.   This feast commemorates the victory of the Jewish people over those who sought to destroy them.   Because of the obedience and daring of Esther and Mordecai, God was able to work to overthrow their enemies.   Although I don't celebrate the Jewish festivals, this one holds a special place in my heart.

When my daughter was born 13 weeks prematurely, I was already caring for my two year old. The twice daily trips to the hospital, and the rollercoaster of emotions as Ellen hung between life and death sapped all my energy and left me feeling unable to cope.   When Ellen finally came home from hospital three months later, she was still desperately sick.   She would stop breathing six or eight times in every twenty-four hours, and I would have to get her started again.   If she failed to breathe adequately again, it meant an emergency dash to hospital for her to be given oxygen.

It took two and a half hours to feed her, which had to be done six times a day – that accounted for fifteen out of every twenty-four hours.   Nonetheless, she failed to thrive.   In desperation I cried out to God as never before, and he answered me in two ways. Firstly, the ladies from my church rallied round and organised a rota, so that every day I had people coming in to do cleaning, cooking, washing and ironing, leaving me free to see to my children. Secondly, I read something that changed my life forever.

I had grown up with the feeling that God had to love me because that was His nature, and that He tolerated me as long as I kept my head down in some obscure corner of His kingdom; and I felt utterly worthless. One day I read an article in which the author quoted from Psalm 66 "For you, God, tested us; you refined us like silver. You brought us into prison and laid burdens on our backs. You let people ride over our heads; we went through fire and water, but you brought us to a place of abundance." He described a prolonged and traumatic experience and explained that through it he had come into such a place of closeness to God that it was worth all he had been through to reach such a place of abundance. I knew it was what I wanted and I prayed possibly the first really sincere prayer I had ever prayed: "God, I don't care what it takes or what I have to go through, please get me to that place of abundance."

Ellen grew weaker and sicker, and at five months old weighed only four pounds fourteen ounces. We were later to discover that her very premature start in life had left her with severe cerebral palsy and autism. The cerebral palsy affected all four of her limbs, her sitting balance and – crucially – her sucking and swallowing muscles, accounting for the feeding difficulties. But at the time I didn't know this. One day, after another exhausting night of trying to feed her and starting her breathing again several times, it suddenly occurred to me that if I smothered her with a pillow, no one would know. They would just think that she had stopped breathing again and I had failed to get to her in time – which the doctors thought was the likely outcome anyway.

With hindsight I was suffering from serious post-natal depression. But I reasoned that this episode could all be over, we could have another baby, and no one would suspect a thing. I was on the stairs, on my way up to fetch a pillow, when there was a ring at the doorbell. I answered the door.

My housegroup leader's wife stood there looking a bit sheepish. She explained that she didn't really know why she had come, she had just had a strong feeling that God was telling her I was in trouble and she should get round here now. I broke down and told her what I had been about to do. She put the children and me into her car, took us to her house, tucked me up in bed and looked after my girls for me.

Afterwards I was amazed that God (a) knew what I was about to do, and (b) cared enough to stop me. It was my first real glimpse of His love and care for me. A few days later I was reading Psalm 45 and verses 10-11 leapt off the page at me: "Listen o daughter, consider and give ear. Forget your people and your father's house. The King is enthralled by your beauty. Honour Him, for He is your Lord."

I saw immediately that God was telling me to forget the ideas of Him that I'd grown up with, and to understand that when He looks at me, He is enthralled by what He sees, and longs for me to feel the same way about Him. I look back on that moment now as the pivotal turning-point in my Christian life. That realisation changed everything and brought me into that place of abundance that I had been longing for. Life continued to be very hard, but God's love was like a secret spring inside me which gave me the strength to cope with it all and to live joyfully.

What has all this to do with the feast of Purim? Years later, I decided to set up Lifeline, a community project from my church giving to other families the same kind of help and support that the ladies from my church had given me. I contacted the local hospital's Special Care Baby Unit, spoke to the doctors and health visitors, and recruited a team of volunteers and a prayer team, ready to support families with seriously ill newborn babies. We have now been running for 14 years, and helped around100 families.

One day when I was starting to set all this up, I was driving along in the car, and thinking about how the very thing the devil had intended for harm – my daughter's fragile start in life and severe disabilities – was being turned around and used against the devil. We were going to bring the love of Jesus to suffering families in a way that would not have happened if the devil hadn't done what he did to Ellen.

I said to God, as I drove along, "There must be an example in Scripture where someone takes something the enemy has intended for their destruction, and uses it to destroy the enemy." Immediately He reminded me of Esther 7. That chapter begins with Haman building a gallows, seventy-five feet high, on which to hang Mordecai, and because of Esther's obedience and God's intervention, it ends with Haman swinging from his own gallows.

It seemed the perfect metaphor for Lifeline. One day I will see people in heaven who wouldn't have been there if the devil hadn't done what he did to Ellen. Like Esther and Mordecai with Haman, it's my mission to hoist the devil with his own petard.

Can I encourage you to do this too? Take a look at what the devil has thrown into your life, things he intended to bring you down and do you harm. Then look around for someone else who is going through something similar, reach out to them with the healing love of Jesus, and watch the devil swing from his own gallows.

5. I only do what I see my Father doing

"I only do what I see my Father doing." This was the one guiding principle of Jesus' life. It explains why, at the Pool Bethesda, He singled out one man from the many and healed him. It explains why, when the rich young ruler walked away, He let him go and didn't chase after him. Given the thousands of people clamouring for His attention, this one principle must have saved Him an awful lot of stress and wasted effort.

I want to try to learn to follow Him in this and live my life this way, too. At the end of last year, it became apparent through a combination of circumstances, words of prophecy, and God's signature peace all over the decision, that it was right for me to give up my job and turn my energies to writing (I have always written, but it has never been my main occupation before). I had no illusions that I could earn a full time living from it, and as a single parent I need to earn a living. But it really was the direction in which God was leading me, and one of the prophecies I received specifically mentioned not worrying about my income but trusting God to provide. So it was to be a big faith venture too, and that really excited me, casting my all on God and letting Him provide for me as a loving Father does.

No sooner had I resigned my job than the publisher of my first book telephoned me and by the end of the conversation I had agreed to write 3 more textbooks and at least 4, possibly 6, compilation books of topical articles linked to the A level Philosophy and Ethics syllabus. This, too, had God's signature peace all over it.

I sent out 7 magazine articles and proposals for articles, and 6 of them were immediately accepted. I put my details onto several freelancing websites, and before long I was receiving offers of work or invitations to bid for work. 3 friends also approached me about either writing books for them or co-authoring books with them. Exciting stuff, but I couldn't manage it all – especially as I was already well on the way with writing a book I felt God had given me to write. I decided to try to apply Jesus' principle. Every time I was offered work, I asked, "Father, is this something You're doing? Do you want me to get involved in this one?" I only accepted the work if I sensed His "yes".

Interestingly, apart from the educational books, most of the projects I felt He has said yes to are ones that will probably not earn me much if anything at all. I'm not worried by this – I've spent the last year wide-eyed in wonder at His ability to provide for me supernaturally. All he's calling me to do is to be obedient.

On Thursday, the Association of Christian Writers' Facebook page was buzzing with a thread that ended up with over 100 posts. Someone had posted a blog from a Christian publisher which said that it's no longer acceptable to offer a book to a publisher and expect him or her to market it. Even before the book proposal is offered, authors need to have built their own platform. In practice that means you need to have 2,000 followers of your blog and on Twitter and Facebook, to convince the publisher that you have a fan base who will buy your book, and that he will get a return on his investment. We all frantically began following each other on Twitter. From having hardly used my Twitter account and having one follower, I started tweeting hectically like everyone else and picked up another 14 followers.

Then I paused and thought: I haven't asked the Father if this is something I see Him doing. I spent part of Friday morning in stillness and silence, listening out for the still, small voice amid the clamour. Very clearly, I heard Him say, "Do not submit again to a yoke of slavery."

On Saturday I went to a writer's day put on by the Association of Christian Writers – the first one I have attended, very enjoyable and worthwhile; I will definitely be going again. Once again, the theme was that we must build a platform, and self-promote in order to promote Christ. I can fully appreciate that publishers need to know, when they take on a book, that it will be profitable and I can entirely understand what was being said, and I don't disagree with it. (Ok, well maybe I do have a little question-mark about it; should Christian publishing be going the way of the world, or should we be saying there is a different, kingdom way of doing this? I just throw the question out; I'm not going to discuss my response to it here.)

But for me, personally, I grew increasingly convinced that this is not what the Father is doing. I can identify with John's words, "I heard a voice from heaven saying, Write." But so far, that's all the voice has said to me. How what I write reaches its intended audience is God's responsibility. If I hear Him tell me to start tweeting frenetically, as He clearly has to some Christian writers, my Twitter profile will spring into life.

But I know that I can only write from the deep spring within me, and in order to keep that replenished and go on having life-giving words to write, I need to spend time by the Well. That's going to mean, for me, that I spend much less, not more, time on Twitter and Facebook. In fact you might find me fairly absent for a time. I'm going to book myself some silent retreat days over the next few weeks and spend much more time with the Man at the Well, letting Him speak His life-giving words into my spirit.

This morning in Church as I thought over my frantic "tweeting" and "following" on Thursday, I had a mental picture of myself putting on running shoes to rush around "building my platform". But when I paused to listen to that still small voice beyond the hubbub around me, I heard Him telling me to take off my shoes and spend some time just standing in adoration on holy ground. So, unlike some of my friends, I haven't given up Facebook for Lent; nevertheless, I may be rather absent for a time. I'll be standing, unshod, staring into a burning bush and hearing a voice out of it. Or I'll be sitting at the Well, listening to One who offers me a well inside me, springing up to eternal life. I have no idea how I'll get my work published, or where this journey will take me. But I suspect I may have something more worth saying for having taken the time to listen to my Father.

6. The World According to Ellen

Like a lot of autistic people, Ellen finds the world a scary and unpredictable place. The rest of us live by rules, but they are rules which Ellen doesn't understand and she hasn't worked out how to predict what they might be.

For example, banging a drum makes an interesting booming noise. Banging a tambourine makes an interesting tinkling noise. And banging another person makes them go, "Ow!" which is a very interesting noise. You are usually allowed to do the first two of these. But someone usually stops you if you try to do the third one. Ellen has no idea why this is. And if you are not allowed to bang another person, what else might you be forbidden to bang? A teapot? A cat? A banana? Ellen has no way of working out the answer to this question.

Occasionally Ellen will see her sisters play-fighting. They seem to be banging each other and I, maker of the rules at home, don't try to stop them. So now apparently the rules have changed and Ellen has absolutely no idea why. It's this failure to understand the principles governing everyone else's behaviour that makes the world such a frightening place for people like Ellen.

So in an attempt to make the world safe and controllable, Ellen imposes some rules of her own. For example, if we go out for dinner, she will only have chicken nuggets and chips. There are plenty of other foods she likes. Some she likes better than chicken nuggets and chips. But she knows that if she always chooses the same thing, eating out will be a safe and predictable experience.

She tries always to do the same activities. Different activities can take place on different days as long as each one is always on the same day of the week and Ellen has a calendar clearly showing them.

We must do certain things only at certain times of the year. Ellen loves me to take her swimming, but it has to be in the October half term holiday. If I suggest a swimming trip in any other month, there is an extreme and negative reaction. We must visit Granny only in the summer holiday or at Christmas. On Friday when I suggested visiting Granny next day, Ellen started hitting herself and shouting that she wanted to go back to the previous weekend (although she surprised me by changing her mind on Saturday morning and coming with me after all!)

Wherever we go – shops, restaurant, hospital, zoo, swimming pool, theme park – she must go and play with the hand dryer in the disabled loo. This again gives every outing a predictability and makes the world a safer place. Hand dryers are predictable. Ellen can understand how they work. People do very unexpected and alarming things, but hand dryers always do exactly the same thing. Press the switch or put your hand under the sensor and this will switch on a motor which drives a fan round, which blows air over a heating element and comes out as a stream of hot air accompanied by a very gratifying noise. And they do this reliably, every time. They never do anything unexpected.

There are 3 words we try to avoid with Ellen because they provoke a very extreme reaction, often involving a damaging degree of self-harm: new, different and change. Birthdays and Christmas are anxious times for her. She loves opening presents, loves the excitement involved and the surprise. But if the present contains something unfamiliar she becomes very distressed. It's new, different and a change. So we give her the same things every time – chocolate, bubble bath, a personal stereo or Dictaphone, bubble wrap. She gets though several rolls of bubble wrap a month. Bubble wrap is predictable and therefore safe. It always behaves in exactly the same way and makes exactly the same noise when you pop it.

The emotional pain arising from an unpredictable change can be, for Ellen, quite literally unbearable. Something has to be done, at once, to make the world feel safe again. The only way is to replace this unmanageable emotional pain with a manageable physical one. That is why Ellen self-harms, sometimes with catastrophic consequences – she has lost all the sight in one eye and more than 50% in the other as a result. It might look like a temper-tantrum, but it isn't. It's a frantic attempt to make this scary, unsafe world seem safe and controllable again.

Last week I took Ellen to the garden centre. This is her favourite outing. She always has chips in the cafe. But this time we arrived early, while they were still serving breakfast. They weren't yet frying chips. The lady behind the counter explained this to Ellen, and suddenly Ellen found herself plunging into a vortex of unpredictability and danger. The world was no longer a safe place where you could go to the garden centre and know that you would be able to have chips. Ellen set up a loud wail and began biting her hand and wrist and punching herself in the face and head. Thank God for a kind and understanding employee in the cafe. She went and had a word with the chef and he agreed to cook chips especially for Ellen – crisis over!

I have come to the conclusion that deep in the soul of every one of us there is a bit that reacts to unpredictability the way Ellen does. We need to know that there is something in the world that never changes and can always be relied on.

I deal with change pretty well. I like things to be different, and I get bored with routine. I like spontaneity – getting up in the morning and deciding to do something I hadn't thought of until that moment, or packing a bag on a whim and going away for a weekend. I like surprises, the more unexpected the better. Yet even I have this core somewhere inside me that needs to know there is something predictable that makes the world safe.

In the last two years I have survived a lifequake. I have lost my marriage, my job, the home where I lived for over 20 years, and have had to learn to do things I've never had to do in my life before – financial planning, self-assessed tax, booking holidays, diy, gardening. I'm loving it! I'm finding a confidence I've never known before from discovering that I can do things I didn't know I could do. Nonetheless, somewhere very deep inside me is a bit that longs for the unchanging.

In particular, I have wanted God not to change. I was quite confident that He wouldn't. After all, didn't He say, "I am the Lord, I change not"? But then, a God who doesn't change and who champions marriage throughout the Bible would save my marriage, right? He would protect my children from the emotional damage involved, right? Like Ellen's frantic behaviour, some of my prayers and some of my conversations with counsellors were desperate attempts to make God predictable and controllable.

But God is far more expansive than my understanding of Him. He refuses to be squashed into my box. Some of my internal struggling looked very like Ellen's self-harm. Some of my incessant bleating (usually by email) was very like her loud wailing. Suddenly the world was unpredictable, and so was God, and it all felt very, very unsafe. What's more, there was nothing I could do to control it or make it safer.

Now that the dust has settled, though, I have discovered that there is something that never changes, and yes, it is God. My understanding of Him has, at times, proved wildly wide of the mark. My vision of Him has been far narrower than the reality. His capacity to surprise me is infinite, and I keep having to revise and adjust my image of Him. But still, He has been the solid rock beneath my feet, and though the lifequake has tossed me high in the air and even upside down at times, I have always come back down with that solid rock immovably in place, and discovered that the world is safer than I ever dreamed – the worst can happen, without destroying me or my children. And out of it all the most serendipitous discovery has come – God really is Love, and I am far, far more loved than ever I realised. I feel more loved than I have ever done at any time in my life. And that makes the world a very safe place indeed.

7. My Love is a Garden Enclosed

Gardening has never appealed to me, for two reasons. One, I am essentially lazy and it looks like hard work. And two, every house we've ever lived in has come with a mature garden, already planted out with lawns, borders, trees and shrubs. There has been no scope for design or imagination.

But for the first time I have moved into a house which is solely mine, and I can do what I like with it. And crucially, it came with a virgin garden. The previous owner had not attempted to do anything with it. The back garden consisted of a patio which has been built too high and breaches the damp course (so it has to go) and a scrubby patch of grass and weeds extending from one fence to the other. The south-west facing front garden consisted of a paved area surrounded by a six-foot hedge that formed a barricade, cutting me off from feeling part of the community.

Suddenly finding myself presented with a more or less blank canvas, gardening has taken on a new appeal. I moved in on 30th September, so I have had all winter to think about what I would do with it. First, I bought a compost bin. Next I mowed the back garden (the grass and weeds were 12 inches high) and overseeded it. I began filling the compost bin with grass cuttings and vegetable peelings. Then I had the top four feet lopped off the hedge so that I now feel as if I belong to the neighbourhood.

I set aside a patch below the kitchen window for vegetables, although I have not yet weeded and planted this. The week before last I went along the two back fences digging out flower borders. I put in some seeds of night-scented stock and giant sunflowers, and was excited to see the first cotyledons appearing above the soil yesterday. Then I bought some bedding plants – phlox, nicotiana and polyanthus and put them in. I have some tubers ready to plant next month. Apart from the polyanthus, all the flowers I have selected have wonderful scents, so that even if Ellen can't see my garden very well, she can still appreciate the fragrance. I bought a trellis and fixed it to the wall of my outhouse, and planted a honeysuckle to grow up it. I bought a large container and put strawberry plants in it.

I had plans to plant a Peace rose in the front garden where it will benefit from the sun. I love Peace – my mother grew it in the garden of my childhood. I love its colours, its scent, and the story of how it got its name (http://www.bexrose.org.uk/RoseArticlePeace.htm). There is only one patch of soil in my front garden, and it was covered in scruffy grass and stones. I went to dig it out and found it was only an inch deep, with flagstones under the soil. Clearly the rose could not go there. I looked for a suitable spot in the back garden, and the only place where the soil was deep enough was in full shade – no good for a rose that loves the sun. So I went to the garden centre and bought a large wooden planter, set it in the front garden, filled it with soil and compost and planted my rose right where I originally planned. I thought it would look lost in the middle of the large container, so I bought a dozen blue petunias and planted them around it – I imagine they will look stunning against the creamy yellow tinged with pink of the Peace rose. Now I am weeding, watering and waiting, expecting a colourful and aromatic display front and back.

I have long loved the imagery of the garden. Even when I was not interested in gardening I still loved gardens, especially ones with varieties of open, sunny areas, hidden shady corners, trees, shrubs, flowers and fruit. Back in 1996 when I heard Chris Bowater using the garden as a symbol of worship, I immediately engaged with the idea.

He said that when we are in the congregation of the church, worshipping Jesus together, it's like going for a walk with Him in the public garden, in the company of His friends. And when we worship Him on our own in privacy and intimacy, it's like taking a walk alone with Him in our own secret garden. As it says in the Song of Songs, "My love is a garden enclosed". I was gripped by this imagery and it transformed my times of personal worship. I could clearly visualise my own secret garden in my mind's eye, and I loved to take walks there hand in hand with my Lord and Lover. I often wrote poems as my natural expression of love to Him during these times, and as they grew in number, I titled the collection "Poems in the Secret Garden".

Making my own first foray into gardening has really enriched my understanding of this picture. I look back on the barren wasteland of my early times of walking with Jesus, and I can see just how much weeding, fertilising and planting He has done. Not that He has imposed these on me – it has been a process of co-operation, learning to love what He loves and knowing that He appreciates those things that I have decided to plant in order to delight Him. I can see how some things in my life which have been culled and rotted away have become the fertiliser for beautiful new things. Where there has not been enough soil for Him to plant the beauty that He wanted to see, He has put structures in place which can hold deep soil and there He has planted the things He wanted to grace the garden. Between us we have redirected streams to irrigate dry areas, and life has sprung out of barrenness. He has done this with my agreement and co-operation. There are still barren areas, weedy areas, stony areas and shallow areas. But little by little He is completing the work He began, and I am enjoying my walks with Him in the romance and intimacy of a place that I share with Him alone.

In all my asking, can it really be
that answers come, not at my own request;
that I am Yours because You asked for me,
and I petition You at Your behest?
In all my seeking, Lord, it's You who seek.
I'm in my garden with just one intent:
to seek Your face, to wait and hear You speak;
but, being sought by You, I am content.
I knock, and know the opening of the door
is promised; but You also knock, to see
if my heart, now ajar, will open more.
There's nothing that originates with me.
Repentance is pre-empted by Your pardon,
and You, not I, designed this secret garden.

8. Nothing Else Matters

The sun's first pale rays spill in through the window-hole near the top of the wall, but I am ahead of him; I've already been up for some time. So has my sister, although it's not her I'm thinking of as I look around our simple home. I stare at the mud floor, little bees of excitement buzzing in my chest as I tell myself, "Today He will be here, in this room, standing on this floor." He will be here.

My sister is impatiently sweeping the floor. I hear the rhythmic whisper of the bristles which seem to echo, "He will be here. He will be here." She taps my feet with the broom in a gesture of annoyance to let me know I'm in the way. I step aside, but today nothing can mar my happiness or discompose me. He is coming.

"Here," she says, "Do something useful. Take this and go and get some water." And she thrusts the earthen waterpot into my hands. Swinging it up onto my head, I start down the dusty path towards the village well. The melody of a song thrush rises above the distant calls of the traders on the way to market. My eye is caught by a flash of colour, and I watch as a bee-eater swoops down the hillside in front of me. Its flight takes it over a patch of poppies and field scabious and I find myself drawn in their direction.

I've heard Him talk about the field flowers, how they don't toil or spin, or busy themselves in any of the ways my sister does, and yet our Father clothes them, better than Solomon in all his glory. He teaches us to call God our Father. I would never have dared to use so intimate a term, but on His lips it just sounds natural and right. I decide to gather a bouquet of the flowers I know He loves. They will make our home welcoming for Him. Setting down the waterpot I pluck the flowers with my right hand and cradle them in my left arm, until I have enough for an ostentatious display on our dining table.

I hurry back to the house to put them in water. But of course there is no water, and my sister scolds me for coming back with no waterpot. "Where did you leave it?" she demands.

"By the path at the edge of the field," I reply, "I'll go and fetch the water now."

"Don't bother," she retorts. "It will be quicker if I go myself." And she rushes off in the direction of the field's edge where I left the waterpot. Feeling a little guilty, and that I ought to help, I look around to see what needs doing. But I can't seem to see our little home, in all its chaos and disarray where my sister has been unarranging and rearranging everything. All I can see in my mind's eye is Him. How will our home look with Him in it?

We are not wealthy people; we have no couch. I look at the three-legged stools, all we have to sit on. They are hard and unyielding; there is no comfort in them after a tiring journey. I take off the scarf that covers my hair and neck, folding it over and over into a neat square. It will make a soft cushion for His weary bones, and I place it on one of the stools.

My sister returns with the water. I pour a little into an earthen vase and begin to arrange the poppies and scabious in it, alternating blue and red to bring a splash of cheer into our colourless room. She mixes flour with leaven, water, oil and herbs, lights a fire and leaves the dough to prove. My brother, who has been at work in the field since dawn, calls in, carrying the carcass of a lamb. He has been to the market. Setting it down on the table, he gives me a kiss and a pat on the shoulder and returns to the field.

My sister arranges the lamb carcass on a spit over the fire and gives me the job of turning it. I sit staring at the flames dancing up and lighting the wall and it reminds me of how He brings a light that sets everyone's heart dancing. Today everything reminds me of Him.

She shapes the dough into loaves and arranges them on the coals. The lamb fat drips down on them, turning their surface into a crisply-fried crust, and she turns them and moves them around to ensure even cooking. It's hot work.

Once the loaves are cooked, she sets out wooden plates and beakers on the table and pours wine into jugs. Meanwhile I sit turning the spit and thinking of Him. He's not what you could call a handsome man, and He's not particularly tall, but He always stands out in a crowd. I can't wait for our home to be filled with His presence.

The meat is cooked at last; my sister takes it away to cut it up. The whole house is filled with tantalising smells of roast lamb, herbs and fresh bread. But before I can savour the promise of dinner, the sounds of distant male laughter begin to drift in on the wind, and in a minute more their footsteps are at the door.

I welcome them in and lead Him to the stool I have cushioned for Him. He sits down, stretches out an appreciative hand to touch the flowers and smiles at me. My sister is nowhere to be seen, tucked away behind the curtain that divides the cooking area from the living quarters of our one-roomed house.

The men sit down on the floor at their teacher's feet. I sit with them and listen, enraptured, as He talks of a shepherd who seeks a lost sheep and a Father who seeks true worshippers. Nothing else matters at this moment. He is my whole world, my sun and moon, my stars and planets, my food and drink, my life and breath. He looks so ordinary, and yet there is something so extraordinary about Him – a glory from another world.

Any other rabbi would rebuke me for presuming to sit down with the men and listen to his teaching. But this one accepts me among His disciples as equal to them. I hardly notice this because I am not thinking of me, but only of Him.

Suddenly I am shocked out of my bubble of contentment as surely as if I had been slapped in the face. My sister rushes in, her cheeks flushed, scarf fallen back over her shoulders, hair awry. She pushes through the men around Him and interrupts His flow of words.

"Lord," she almost shrieks, "don't You care that my sister has left me to do all the work by myself? Tell her to help me!"

Guiltily I jump to my feet, but His hand on my shoulder lightly pushes me back into place. He takes my sister by both forearms and gently pulls her down until she is sitting beside me on the floor.

"Martha, Martha," He says as He lowers her down, "you are worried and upset about many things, but only one thing is needed. Mary has chosen what is better, and it will not be taken away from her."

Martha looks round uncertainly, embarrassed to be sitting on the floor among the men. I draw her towards me, kiss the bewilderment from her face, and rest my arm across her shoulders.

"Listen to Him," I whisper to her. "Nothing else matters."

9. Riding the Storm

Psalm 107. 23 – 32
Those who go down to the sea in ships,
Who do business on great waters,
They see the works of the Lord,
And His wonders in the deep.
For He commands and raises the stormy wind,
Which lifts up the waves of the sea.
They mount up to the heavens,
They go down again to the depths;
Their soul melts because of trouble.
They reel to and fro and stagger like a drunken man,
And all their wisdom is swallowed up.
Then they cry out to the Lord in their trouble,
And He brings them out of their distresses.
He calms the storm so that its waves are still.
Then they are glad because they are quiet;
So He guides them to their desired haven.
OH! that men would give thanks to the Lord for His goodness
And for His wonderful works to the children of men!
Let them exalt Him also in the assembly of the people,
And praise Him in the company of the elders.
v.43
Whoever is wise will observe these things,
And they will understand the loving kindness of the Lord.

When I was in my teens I loved sailing. Some kinds of sailing more than others – dinghy sailing was good fun in its way, tacking across Chichester Harbour, or along the

Helford River in Cornwall. But real exhilaration was being out on the North Sea in a 30-foot Bermuda rigged sloop, at the mercy of the elements, harnessing the wind and navigating a course through the waters by day, and at night anchored in some sheltered creek, lulled to sleep in my wooden bunk by the gentle movement of the waves – nothing beats it for restoration of the soul, and I'm fortunate enough never to have experienced seasickness.

I remember well an incident when I was just 12 years old. My father ran sailing holidays for young people, and he took me along with him – two weeks of sleeping, cooking and sharing fellowship on board, only putting in to shore when the drinking water ran out or the bread turned mouldy. On this particular day we were crossing the Medway Estuary and heading north up the Essex coast. The shipping forecast predicted ideal conditions for the trip: clear skies, good visibility and winds of force 4 – 5.

We set out in high spirits; the mainsail and jib filled with wind as the bow sliced through the water, leaving a gentle wake trailing behind us. It was such a pleasant, straightforward sail that my father told me to get out my guitar and lead some singing. So I sat in the cockpit with the guitar and we all sang,
"This is the day, this is the day,
That the Lord has made, that the Lord has made.
We will rejoice, we will rejoice
And be glad in it, and be glad in it."

The first thing I noticed was a change in my father's demeanour. Suddenly he became tense and focused on the horizon, all his senses on full alert.

"Put the guitar away!" he ordered, in a tone I didn't question. I quickly stowed it in my cabin and returned on deck. Now we could all see what my father had seen. On the horizon, a well-defined area of dark grey cloud was racing towards us at a speed that had to be seen to be believed, whipping the sea into a frenzy beneath it as it rushed in our direction.

"My father shouted, "Life jackets on!" and we all obeyed. He pointed at me and a young lad named David. "You two – harnesses on!" We strapped the harnesses over our shoulders and around our waists, fastening them securely. "Go and get the mainsail down!" David and I shackled the karabiners on our harnesses to the mast and began to lower the mainsail.

My father was an absolute stickler for having everything on board ship, well.... shipshape; every item put away, every rope neatly coiled, and the sails smoothly and evenly furled. David and I began to furl the sail meticulously, as we had been taught. "Forget that!" my father shouted. "Just get it down and tie a bit of rope round it." I was astonished – it was the first time he had ever instructed me not to do something "properly". We let go the sheets and grabbed at the sail, yanking it down as fast as we could, and tying it down roughly. Just as we finished and stood up, the squall slammed into us. I expected it to hit us amid-ships, but while we had been dealing with the sail, my father had turned the yacht directly into the storm, out to sea, to avoid the risk of being driven onshore. The bow of the ship rose up in the air as the first wave raced up underneath it, and then we rushed down the other side of the wave. David and I dared not undo our harnesses from the mast, or we would have been overboard for sure, so we stood there, on the highest point of the deck, hanging onto the mast, with a grandstand view of this magnificent storm.

At 12 I was too young to appreciate the very real danger we were in, and I found the whole experience totally exhilarating. Before long the waves were coming at us from the side, and were as high as the mast. We would hurtle up each wave to the crest, then plunge down into the trough as the next wave towered over us and looked as if it were about to break across our deck. Then at the last moment we would race up that one too, and then plummet down into the next trough. The squall lasted only about 15 minutes, but later that evening we heard on the shipping report that it had been gusting up to hurricane force 11, and I could well believe it.

I don't know how my father felt, responsible as he was for the lives of six young people in his care, but if he was at all perturbed, he never showed it for a moment. He was calm, focused, alert and in control, and his actions brought us safely through that storm with only one minor injury between us. That night, at anchor in the calm once more, we read this passage from Psalm 107.

As my life navigates through some pretty big storms, I often think back to that day. Now, as then, the ship of my life is in the hands of a competent Captain who has made Himself totally responsible for my safety and wellbeing. Sometimes my inclination would be to navigate away from the approaching storm, but He knows that to hug the shoreline is to risk being driven aground and wrecked, and so He turns my bow and points me straight out to face the oncoming hurricane head-on. He harnesses me to a place of safety so that I can never be swept overboard, and He expertly navigates the crests and troughs of the waves, no matter how high and overwhelming they look. I know that He is utterly committed to bringing me into safe harbour, and although all I can now see is the current moment, the ferocity of the storm, and yes, at times the intensity of my fear as the waves threaten to swamp my deck, I know that just a short while from now I will be safely at anchor in a sheltered place, glad because I am quiet, and have been guided to my desired haven.

At any time He could choose to say to the wind and the waves, "Peace! Be still!" But for now He holds back and lets the storm rage. Let it rage. If my vessel were in my hands, I would perish. But I have handed the Captaincy over to Him, and He has a 100% track record. No vessel Captained by Him has ever come to disaster. No wonder the Psalmist longed for everyone to give thanks to Him for His goodness, and for His wonderful works to the children of men. I cannot be swept onto the rocks or swamped by the sea – even if at times it looks close. My destiny is peace and safety – and to sail again another day. "Whoever is wise will observe these things, and they will understand the loving kindness of the Lord."

10. Grace and Glory

John was arguably the person closest to Jesus during His 3 years of ministry. He defined himself as the disciple whom Jesus loved, and it was he who sat closest to Jesus in the intimacy of deep friendship at the Last Supper. And it was John who said of Him, "We beheld His glory, the glory as of the only-begotten of the Father, full of grace and truth."

Reflecting on this lately, it seems to me that the grace of Jesus has to be properly understood against a background of His glory as the one who has pre-eminence over all, over everything in heaven and on earth and under the earth. Just as the rainbow shows up brightest against the darkest of clouds, so the grace of Jesus shines most brightly when we see the magnificence of His glory in full colour.

If God is my Father, or my Shepherd, or my Bridegroom, then – I say this reverently – grace and lovingkindness is to be expected; it is a function of the role. But if He is the supreme King of Kings, to whom all authority is given, who reigns over all that exists, whose government and peace continues to increase eternally, then who am I to expect grace from Him? And yet in the Bible it is often at the moments when His glory is most radiantly revealed that the amazing humility of His grace is shown the most clearly and beautifully.

Take, for example, Ezekiel's vision by the River Chebar. He describes the four living creatures, and this vision alone is stunning enough – but pales by comparison with the One they are worshipping:

"Now above the expanse that was over their heads there was something resembling a throne, like lapis lazuli in appearance; and on that which resembled a throne, high up, was a figure with the appearance of a man. Then I noticed from the appearance of His loins and upward something like glowing metal that looked like fire all around within it, and from the appearance of His loins and downward I saw something like fire; and there was a radiance around Him. As the appearance of the rainbow in the clouds on a rainy day, so was the appearance of the surrounding radiance. Such was the appearance of the likeness of the glory of the LORD. And when I saw it, I fell on my face and heard a voice speaking."

The only possible response Ezekiel can make is to fall to the ground. This is not even a voluntary response – it is the inevitable reaction of frail flesh in the presence of eternal and infinite Majesty. He is overwhelmed by the vision and the presence of Almighty God and can only fall down in worship and wonder to the dust of earth where he stands.

The voice which speaks to him gives him an utterly impossible instruction: "Son of man, stand to your feet so that I can speak with you!" It is beyond Ezekiel's ability to raise himself up and stand eye-to-eye with the Eternal God. And God knows this, and so with tender humility His Spirit stoops to the ground where Ezekiel lies and enters him, to raise him to his feet.

The picture is even more graphic in Revelation 1 when John encounters his dear Friend, now risen, ascended and glorified. This is the Jesus on whose bosom John rested his head in His final hours, who heard His last words to His disciples, who was one of the three who witnessed His agony in the Garden of Gethsemane and was close enough to hear and record His high-priestly prayer. Had he encountered Him again just as He was in the days of His flesh, surely he would have embraced Him and resumed the old, affectionate familiarity. But the vision of Jesus is so different. Yes, in His flesh John has already glimpsed that glory, full of grace and truth, but now he encounters the full force of it:

"Then I turned to see the voice that was speaking with me. And having turned I saw seven golden lampstands; and in the middle of the lampstands I saw one like a son of man, clothed in a robe reaching to the feet, and girded across His chest with a golden sash. His head and His hair were white like white wool, like snow; and His eyes were like a flame of fire. His feet were like burnished bronze, when it has been made to glow in a furnace, and His voice was like the sound of many waters. In His right hand He held seven stars, and out of His mouth came a sharp two-edged sword; and His face was like the sun shining in its strength."

And his reaction to his dear Friend is exactly the same as Ezekiel's. Even John, who has willingly forsaken all and endured unbelievable hardship, persecution and loneliness for the love of his precious Lord is overwhelmed by the presence of His glory: "When I saw Him, I fell at His feet like a dead man." Nothing too astonishing about that, given the description he has just written of the appearance of the Lord Jesus. What is really astonishing is the next verse: "And He placed His right hand on me and said…."

This is the picture: the Lord Jesus, resplendent in a radiance that outshines the noonday sun in the Middle East, appears in His surpassing majesty. John, overwhelmed by the Presence, falls down into the dust beneath his feet and lies there like a dead man. And this risen Lord who stands towering over him, places His right hand on him. How does He do that? The only way it's possible is that He stoops and gets right down in the dust and dirt where John lies, and with utmost tenderness, lays a hand of love on him in an act of staggering humility.

And isn't this what I also experience in my daily life? It's so easy to take the grace of God for granted. He's my Father, my Shepherd, my Guide, even my Helper – this is what I expect of Him. But catch one true glimpse of His real glory and magnificence, however dimly, and suddenly His grace is breathtaking – that He should stoop right down here among all the messiness and untidiness and grubbiness that is my life – that He who reigns in splendour above the highest heavens should sit in the dirt beside me and place a hand of the gentlest tenderness on me to lift me up out of the dust… that's when I begin to see a faint and distant gleam of the grace and glory of my Lord Jesus and I am lost for words at the height and depth and breadth and length of such an undeserved yet unstintingly given love. How wonderful He is, how inadequate my words to praise Him!

11. Acceptable in the sight of my Redeemer

This afternoon I visited Winchester Cathedral to enable my daughter Natasha to complete some drawings for a project on religious art. While we were there I went, as I always do, to make my pilgrimage to the tomb of Jane Austen. She is probably one of the writers who has most influenced me. Whether or not you enjoy her stories, no one can deny that she is a past-master at creating lifelike characters.

I read once again the familiar inscription on her tombstone, and noted, as I always do, how its final paragraph grated on me. But it struck me today – Easter Saturday – that this weekend of all weekends, there is a good reason for pondering those words and asking if they ring true.

Here is the inscription:

In Memory of Jane Austen, youngest daughter of the late Revd George Austen, formerly Rector of Steventon in this County. She departed this Life on the 18th of July 1817, aged 41, after a long illness supported with the patience and the hopes of a Christian.

The benevolence of her heart, the sweetness of her temper, and the extraordinary endowments of her mind obtained the regard of all who knew her and the warmest love of her intimate connections.

Their grief is in proportion to their affection, they know their loss to be irreparable, but in their deepest affliction they are consoled by a firm though humble hope that her charity, devotion, faith and purity have rendered her soul acceptable in the sight of her Redeemer.

To these accolades we could add her faithful trust in God throughout dashed hopes of love and marriage, and her patient fortitude in the face of a painful, prolonged and early death, possibly due to Addison's disease. But whenever I read this, I ask myself whether it was Jane's "charity, devotion, faith and purity" (irrefutable though they were) that rendered her acceptable in the sight of her Redeemer. And in the Easter story, I believe we have the answer.

Crucified alongside the Lord Jesus there were two thieves. One of them, by his own account, was being crucified "justly, for we are receiving what we deserve for our deeds". He had nothing to recommend him to Jesus; certainly nothing that could be described as "charity, devotion, faith and purity".

In fact, he had only three things going for him. One was that he knew his need. He did not try to stand on his own merits, because he knew that he had none. He had lived a life of dishonesty and very probably violence. So heinous were his crimes, he acknowledged that he deserved to die. Secondly, he recognised the holiness and sinlessness of the man on the cross next to him: "but this man has done nothing wrong." And thirdly, he had faith and believed that this was no ordinary man, but a King whose reign would extend even beyond the jurisdiction of death, and so he asked, "Jesus, remember me when You come in Your kingdom!"

Jesus' response might have been, "After the life you've lived? You have GOT to be joking!" If personal virtues like Jane Austen's were necessary to make us acceptable to our Redeemer, this is what He would have had to reply. But see what He actually said, without hesitation: "Truly I say to you, today you shall be with Me in Paradise." This is not just good news; this is absolutely amazing news for people who, like me, have not attained Jane Austen's heights of saintliness. Even without a catalogue of good deeds, this man was acceptable to God, not because of what He had done, but because of what his King was doing at that very moment.

St Paul tells us that God has made us "accepted in the Beloved" (Ephesians 1.6) In other words, I'm accepted not because I have done enough to make myself acceptable to my Redeemer, but because Jesus is the Father's Beloved, and has done everything necessary on my behalf. In fact, Paul even goes so far as to say that on the cross Jesus exchanged my sinfulness for His righteousness: "For He made Him who knew no sin to be sin for us, that we might become the righteousness of God in Him." (2 Corinthians 5.21)

I am well aware that I fall short of the example of Christian living that I see when I read biographies of Jane Austen. I also think I maybe compare pretty favourably with the thief who was crucified next to Jesus. But thank God, I am not assessed in relation to either of these standards. I am acceptable to my Redeemer because He made me, and He loved me enough to rescue me by giving me His own righteousness, even when I had fallen hopelessly short of His glory.

It's a popular slogan, but it's nonetheless true: Jesus thinks I'm to die for.

12. Wheat and tares

My first ever foray into the world of gardening is beginning to pay off. The flower borders are starting to unfold into a display of yellow and red. The vegetable seeds I sowed and covered with poly tunnels are just poking up through the soil. I was very dubious about my ability to grow brassicas successfully, but the Brussels sprouts plants I put in are strong and flourishing. The Peace rose is putting out new shoots, so are the phlox, and the bedding plants are growing healthily. The nematodes I watered in seem to have dealt with the slugs; the honeysuckle which was a spindly eighteen inches when I planted it is now four feet high and bushing upwards and outwards against the trellis which I fixed to the outhouse wall. The night-scented stock and sunflower seeds are starting to germinate in the borders. The sweet peas are creeping up the canes I placed for their support. The grass is thickening up where I overseeded it, the birds are coming regularly to my bird table, and when I sit at my desk or run on my treadmill I survey my little domain with a real sense of satisfaction, and anticipation of the coming summer months when I will be able to sit out and relax in it (if it ever stops raining!)

There's just one problem. When I moved here six months ago the lawn was twelve inches high and consisted as much of dandelions, buttercups, dock leaves and stinging nettles as of grass. I covered it with weed and feed and the weeds have started to die back, but not before leaving last season's seeds all over the garden. In all the flower borders cotyledons are beginning to open out on the surface of the soil and I find it impossible to tell which ones are the seeds I planted and which are the weeds. At this stage they look so similar that I don't have the confidence to start weeding them out for fear of uprooting the plants I'm hoping will fill my borders by the summer.

I'm reminded of Jesus' parable of the wheat and the tares. "The kingdom of heaven may be compared to a man who sowed good seed in his field. But while his men were sleeping, his enemy came and sowed tares among the wheat, and went away. But when the wheat sprouted and bore grain, then the tares became evident also. The slaves of the landowner came and said to him, 'Sir, did you not sow good seed in your field? How then does it have tares?' And he said to them, 'An enemy has done this!' The slaves said to him, 'Do you want us, then, to go and gather them up?' But he said, 'No; for while you are gathering up the tares, you may uproot the wheat with them. Allow both to grow together until the harvest; and in the time of the harvest I will say to the reapers, "First gather up the tares and bind them in bundles to burn them up; but gather the wheat into my barn." (Matthew 13. 24-30)

This is one of Jesus' parables of the end times, looking ahead to what will happen when He returns to establish His reign of justice and peace. But like so many of Jesus' stories, it has different layers of meaning. I look at my own life, and I can see some things which God has planted and which are flourishing. I see other things which, frankly, are shrivelling up and need a good watering from the well of the Holy Spirit. But I also see new things beginning to germinate. Some of them worry me. Is this one a trait God wants me to develop? Is it something He's going to use in my life? Is it going to grow into something that bears fruit from which others can be fed? Or is it something insidious that will spread its roots invisibly around the things God wants to grow and choke them? It's not always easy to tell. Am I becoming less anxious, more restful, more trusting of God? Or is my natural tendency to laziness reasserting itself when I should be expending energy in pursuit of what God wants for my life? It can sometimes be hard to distinguish. Am I learning to relate to God in everyday life instead of religiously following the patterns of my upbringing (e.g. you must get up early every morning to have a "quiet time" – this is the foundation of Christian living)? Or can I just not be bothered to get up early and spend that time with Him at present? Am I becoming more sensitive in my dealings with those who don't yet know Jesus personally? Or have I lost my passion and boldness in sharing the Gospel?

At the moment these are questions I genuinely don't know the answers to. Some of them could be applied to the church, too. As God gently dismantles the structures we have been used to in church life and shows us a new way to be as the Body of Christ, He is sowing many new seeds that are going to result in greater fruitfulness, increased unity and love, deeper maturity. But in among all of that there are bound to be some things that will not be helpful, new ideas that don't move us on in our journey from vision to reality. And it can be very hard to distinguish one from the other. It would be very easy to go round uprooting things left, right and centre, both in my own life and in the life of the church, with the attendant risk that we remove or damage the burgeoning seedlings that God wants to grow in us – or worse still, remove His sowings and leave the weeds to flourish.

I'm itching to start ripping things out of the soil in my flower borders, but I'm restraining myself until they grow to the stage where it's obvious what they are and which ones need to be removed. That could take many more weeks yet, and the process takes patience and trust – I have to set aside any anxiety and believe that the weeds will not be allowed to strangle the plants I've sowed. In my life, too, I'm trying to learn to trust things into God's hands and wait patiently for the moment when He begins to say, "Now you can see why that one is not helpful and needs to come out, and now you can see why that one is going to be a real blessing to you and others and needs to be watered and fed." In the meantime, I have to listen to Him, allow His rain to water my life, drawing constantly from His well of supply, and basking in the sunshine of His presence. Soon enough it will start to become apparent what adjustments I need to make and what I need to abandon in order to pursue His agenda. The same is true in church life – we can trust the Holy Spirit to show us when and how to uproot something that's growing where it doesn't belong, and how best to water the emergent fruits that will turn His church into a source of beauty and nourishment for the community in which He has placed us.

13. Word Perfect.

There were sounds a-plenty, but none that could be called speech; it was hard to tell if they signified anything. As she grew from baby to toddler, I was convinced that she could understand, even if she couldn't respond or initiate conversation. If I said, "Close the door," she would roll across the floor and push it shut with her little body. This gave me real hope that perhaps the doctors were wrong, and she had more intelligence than they had thought.

The first hint of her musical ability came at a very early stage. She would sit in her bouncing cradle, staring expressionlessly into the distance, humming frère Jacques, the tune played by the toy on her cot. What I didn't appreciate then, and only realised later, was that she was humming it in the same key as the toy on her cot.

The "wow" moment came the first time she encountered a piano. She was two years old. She poked the keys tentatively with her good hand, listening to the sounds they made. And then without hesitation, she played frère Jacques, note-perfect, still in that same key. After that I was determined to unlock whatever was inside her.

Teachers came to the house every week to help me do it. We decided to tackle numbers. Although she still didn't speak, she could soon point to piles of the right quantity of bricks when given a number from one to five. Next we decided to try colours. For a week she was only allowed to wear red clothes, only allowed to play with red toys, only allowed to paint red pictures and only allowed to eat red food. We were big on tomatoes and strawberries that week, although it's amazing what you can do with a bottle of cochineal – red rice, red custard, red mashed potato..... Week by week we worked through the colours, and soon she could select the asked-for colour from a variety that we offered.

It wasn't until she was five that the words began to come. The first word she ever spoke was "cake"! That was followed by "dad". Monosyllables were all she managed for a long time.

Many painful operations took their toll, and she became frightened and withdrawn. We arranged music therapy, and she relaxed and let go of the fear as she learned to express through music the emotions she couldn't articulate in words. Her first full sentence came one summer's day when the door bell rang and I said, "Here's Jenny come to do music with you." She waved her good arm excitedly and shouted, "I love you!"

One of my happiest moments followed not long after. Her older sister was teasing her mercilessly, and, unable to get up and leave as any other child could have done, she lay there growing increasingly annoyed. Finally the frustration had to erupt, and she shouted, "Shut your face!" It was so appropriate in the context that I knew, whatever the doctors said, that the wordless exterior concealed a lively intelligence.

One day she came home from school and hesitatingly, haltingly, began to recite a nursery rhyme she had learned. I realised that if she could memorise nursery rhymes, she could memorise God's word. So I sat down in front of her and asked her to repeat a verse after me, phrase by phrase.

"You have," I said.

"You have," she repeated.

"Delivered," I continued.

"Delivered," she responded obediently.

"My feet," I went on.

And that was when she astonished me. Instead of repeating, "My feet," she finished the verse: "from stumbling." All those years that I had read the Bible to her, she had been taking it in, though she'd had no way of letting me know.

People abort unborn babies just because they have some kind of disability. If you point out that this is just another form of disability discrimination, the argument is sometimes put forward that it isn't fair on the parents to have their lives ruined by having to raise a child with such challenging difficulties. To this I would reply that yes, the difficulties are challenging. But the rewards, when the child achieves something you have been told they will never manage, go way beyond anything parents of simply "normal" children will ever experience. And who are we to deny a baby the chance to climb that mountain of effort and reach adulthood with a far greater sense of achievement than their peers?

14. Meditation for stillness

I spent today at a retreat centre in silence and stillness. Unusually for me, I found it really difficult to stop my mind flitting around all over the place and bring it back to the present. In the end I decided to write down the distractions, and in so doing I found I made use of them to lead me into a place of being present to the present moment, and the inner quiet soon followed. Here is what I wrote:

Make me aware of now,
For my mind is full of then.
Then, when I erred and grieved You;
Then, when I doubted You;
Then, when You reassured me of my acceptance;
Then, when I was wronged and You taught me to forgive.

Make me aware of now,
For my mind is full of then.
Then, when I shall accomplish my dreams;
Then, when my words will shed Your light on someone else's path;
Then, when I will cease to struggle with these besetting sins;
Then, when I will banish all distractions and hold You in my gaze.

Make me aware of now,
For my mind is full of then.
Then, when I will know the things I now try to believe;
Then, when I will feel Your love as truly as I feel my beating heart;

Then, when I will fix my eyes on You and learn never
to turn away;
Then, when the anguish of failure will cease to trouble
my heart.

Make me aware of now,
For my mind is full of then.
Now, when the fly is blundering against the window
pane, ignorant of glass;
Now, when the blackbird in the garden is proudly
calling over and over his full-throated song;
Now when the curling thread of steam from my cup
brings the aroma of coffee to my senses;
Now, when the scratch of this pen on this paper
marks the time signature of my thoughts;
Now, when the rise and fall of my chest settles into
the slow contentment of relaxation.

Make me aware of now,
For my mind is letting go of then.
Now, when the rigidity of this chair holds my reclining
body;
Now, when the radiation from this electric heater
blows the chill from my feet;
Now, when the hymn book open on my Bible is no
longer needed to remind me who You are;
Now, when the stillness of the tall trees and the
movement of the bushes illustrate the differing air
currents.

Make me aware of now,
For my soul is losing interest in then.
Now, when the painted river in its frame above me
speaks Your name – Spirit;
Now, when the distant hillside illustrates Your nature
– Rock;

Now, when these soft cushions cradle me the way
You do – Mother;
Now, when these four walls cast round me a solid
protection like Yours – Father;
Now, when the air I breathe preserves my life as You
do – Saviour;
Now, when the clamour dies away and I begin to hear
the softest of whispers;
Now – speak, Lord; Your servant is listening.

15. Thanks for the memory!

Recently my daughter Natasha was watching a drama on TV in which the protagonist was offered the chance to have her memory erased so that she had no recollection of some bad stuff that had just been happening. I didn't stay in the room to see what happened, so I don't know what choice she made! However, it did get me thinking. Like everyone else, I have my share of good and bad memories. Suppose I could have all the bad ones erased. Would I want to?

I thought back over some of the things that have happened in my life. Among the small frustrations and what Shakespeare called the "thousand natural shocks that flesh is heir to" some stand out as being particularly distressing. Being kidnapped by a soldier from Kneller Hall on my way home from school at the age of 13 (and only by the grace of God escaping with my life). Going into labour months early and giving birth at 27 weeks. Being told my daughter Ellen would never walk and probably didn't have the intelligence ever to learn any speech (I wish that doctor could see her now, writing words into search engines on the computer, and hear her reading the results!) And some more recent traumas which have left me with flashbacks and nightmares, although as time goes on these are lessening.

Suppose all of those things could vanish from my conscious and subconscious mind, leaving only the happy memories? Is that something I would want? As I pondered the question, it didn't take me long to reach a very decisive answer. These things have shaped who I am today, and no, I wouldn't want to forget them. They have been the means of learning just how dependable and unfailing God is, in the middle of a world of uncertainty and insecurity.

For example, I remember the summer of 1996. Ellen, at the age of 12, had just undergone major surgery. The curvature of her spine had become so acute that it was putting pressure on her heart, lungs and stomach. Her breathing was laboured and inefficient, she was pitifully thin from being unable to eat very much and, the doctors told us, she was at imminent risk of heart failure. The operation was very risky and even as I signed the consent form, I was aware that I might well be agreeing to the means of her death. She survived the operation, but it damaged some of the nerves to the lower half of her body. She could no longer crawl, losing her only means of independent mobility, and her legs were greatly weakened, making it hard for her to weight bear even long enough for us to pull up her trousers. But most distressing of all, just as she was becoming a young lady and I was taking her out to buy her first bras, she became doubly incontinent and went back into nappies.

As I grappled with my feelings about all this, I went to talk it over with my pastor. He wisely listened without saying much, allowed me to offload all my feelings and then prayed with me. I went home and switched on the cassette player in my kitchen. The first song that came up was "My Jesus, my Saviour". A phrase from the song leapt out at me: "My comfort, my shelter, tower of refuge and strength". As I heard those words I had an almost tangible, physical sensation of being wrapped around and around in the comfort of God. The presence of Jesus was so very manifest there in my kitchen, and I suddenly understood something for the first time in my life: it's worth absolutely anything we go through just to know that our comfort comes from Jesus. Because if we were never in need of comforting, there's a whole facet of the character of Jesus that we would never experience, and no price is too high to pay to touch those depths of God and experience His love and care.

Then in 2010, after much prayer and agonising, it became clear that it was time to leave a relationship that had become very damaging. God provided temporary accommodation miraculously for Natasha and me. I found a suitable (albeit tiny) bungalow, but the estate agent told me the landlord was a hard-headed businessman who would never accept me as a tenant because my income wasn't adequate for the rent. I was completely at peace about this because I had been praying, "If I'm doing the wrong thing, stop me". The next day the estate agent told me the landlord had signed a waiver allowing me to move in even though I couldn't give any financial guarantees. When I asked why, what was in it for him, she shrugged her shoulders and said, "We don't know, he just said he would!" My salary just covered rent, food and travel to work but nothing else at all and throughout the year we were there God provided miraculously for us again and again. I started out sleeping on a bit of foam on the floor, but was then given 2 excellent quality beds, one of them brand new; I was down to my last £90 and found out that a friend who had died over a year earlier had left me £500 in her will; a pastor's wife came to visit and left me a gift of £100, I had an anonymous gift of £600 and when I ran out of money about 6 weeks before the end of my tenancy I got a tax rebate of £650! When I was a child my parents had made a lifestyle choice to give up a secure and well paid job to work for a Christian charity which involved them having to trust God to provide for their financial needs, and throughout my childhood I had witnessed His provision for our family again and again. But that had been my parents' faith. Now I was having an opportunity to experience His faithfulness at first hand.

So would I erase the memories of everything bad that has happened? Would I forget what it is to be desperately in need of comfort and receive it from Jesus himself? Would I forget the adventure of faith that cast me completely on God for provision? Would I relinquish the inner strength that has come from surviving painful events and coming out stronger, closer to God and more reliant on Him? Not me, I would have pressed the "No" button if I'd been the girl in that TV drama.

A quick search in Bible Gateway reveals that the word "remember" occurs 210 times in the Bible. The phrase "forget not" occurs 8 times. It seems that remembering the past is important to God, but why? Certainly not to dwell on it and wallow in the pain. There seem to be two things that are important in these scriptures. Firstly, to remember our own tendency to stray from God, and how some of the apparently bad things that have happened to us have actually been His loving way of drawing us back to Himself: "Remember how the Lord your God led you through the wilderness for these forty years, humbling you and testing you to prove your character, and to find out whether or not you would obey his commands. Yes, he humbled you by letting you go hungry and then feeding you with manna, a food previously unknown to you and your ancestors. He did it to teach you that people do not live by bread alone; rather, we live by every word that comes from the mouth of the Lord. For all these forty years your clothes didn't wear out, and your feet didn't blister or swell. Think about it: Just as a parent disciplines a child, the Lord your God disciplines you for your own good. So obey the commands of the Lord your God by walking in his ways and fearing him." (Deuteronomy 8. 2-6) And secondly, to remember the terrible plight we were in and then celebrate how God rescued us from it. This in turn will remind us to treat others with the justice and compassion we have received: "There will always be some in the land who are poor. That is why I am commanding you to share freely with the poor and with other Israelites in need. If a fellow Hebrew sells himself or herself to be your servant and serves you for six years, in the seventh year you must set that servant free. When you release a servant, do not send him away empty-handed. Give him a generous farewell gift from your flock, your threshing floor, and your winepress. Share with him some of the bounty with which the Lord your God has blessed you. Remember that you were once slaves in the land of Egypt and the Lord your God redeemed you! That is why I am giving you this command." (Deuteronomy 15. 11-15)

But there is also something which God tells us not to remember: "You will no longer remember the shame of your youth and the sorrows of widowhood. For your Creator will be your husband; the Lord of Heaven's Armies is his name! He is your Redeemer, the Holy One of Israel, the God of all the earth. For the Lord has called you back from your grief—as though you were a young wife abandoned by her husband, says your God. For a brief moment I abandoned you, but with great compassion I will take you back. In a burst of anger I turned my face away for a little while. But with everlasting love I will have compassion on you, says the Lord, your Redeemer."

(Isaiah 54. 4-8) All those memories which we are to recall and not forget, have had the sting drawn from them. God has understood the depth of pain and abandonment we have at times felt, but He wants us to leave behind the shame and the grief. We don't forget all that has happened to us, and we certainly don't forget God's amazing care and faithfulness which have shone like the sun throughout those dark moments. But we don't hold on to the negative feelings which accompanied those times, because we have something to celebrate – God has redeemed us, transformed us and turned our lives around. He has exchanged our spirit of despair and heaviness for a garment of praise.

Bless the Lord, O my soul, and all that is within me, bless His holy name. Bless the Lord, O my soul, and forget none of His benefits; who pardons all your iniquities, who heals all your diseases; who redeems your life from the pit, who crowns you with lovingkindness and compassion; who satisfies your years with good things, so that your youth is renewed like the eagle. (Psalm 103. 1-5)

16. Blissful Ignorance

We had a writers' circle meeting tonight, and in the absence of anything specifically written for the occasion, I read out something I wrote a while ago for the Faithwriters' weekly challenge. The challenge was to write a piece in any genre, between 150 and 750 words on the topic of "predicament". I remarked tonight that I couldn't really think of the purpose of this piece, where I could use it; and the general consensus was that I should publish it as a blog post, so here it is. It is a true story – there is a word of explanation at the end.

I looked at the woman on the other side of my desk, clutching the tiny child on her lap. How much did she really suspect? I wondered. The baby was fifteen months old, and the examination I had just undertaken sent chills down my spine, especially as the mother seemed so untroubled.

I tested the waters. "Do you know why your Health Visitor made this appointment?"

She shrugged. "She was concerned. She thinks she should be doing more by now."

"And what about you? Are you concerned?" I looked at the child, her head turned to one side, elbows tightly bent, fists clenched with the thumbs across the palms, legs scissoring, the total stiffness of her body demonstrating the spasticity of the muscles.

The mother shook her head. "No. She was more than 3 months early. She's been desperately sick for the past fifteen months. Of course she's behind in her development. You'd expect her to be. But I'm not worried. I don't think there's anything wrong with her."

I studied her carefully. How much should I tell her? I had got to know this young lady quite well. This was her second very premature baby in just over two years, and I'd seen more of her than of most of our parents.

I remembered the day I mentioned that the baby had Wilson-Mikity Syndrome. Most parents would have asked me superficial questions and left it at that. Not this one. She said nothing at the time, but came back the next day full of information, facts and figures, using medical terminology with clear understanding. Long before the days of computers, she had evidently been to the public library and sat there until she had committed to memory everything she could find out about Wilson-Mikity Syndrome. She knew it meant her baby could die, and that if she recovered it might take weeks or months. She could cite studies of previous cases. Right then I set her down as someone with an enquiring mind and a lively intelligence.

She was shifting a little uncomfortably in her chair, waiting for me to say something. I had been silent during these reflections, to the point where the silence was becoming awkward. What should I tell her now? She genuinely seemed blithely unaware of the seriousness of her baby's condition. I could not get any of the normal motor responses from the child. Her limbs didn't jerk when I tapped her knees and elbows with the hammer. Her head obstinately refused to go into any position except turned to the right. Her fists would not uncurl, and her arms refused to extend – the left one was far tighter than the right. Already the adductor tendons were showing signs of shortening so that it was becoming difficult to part her legs enough to put her nappy on. There was little sign of recognition or intelligence in her eyes. I was certain the child would never walk. Probably she would never sit up unsupported. I doubted whether she had the intelligence ever to learn any speech.

And here sat her mother, telling me that she expected her daughter to be behind in her development, and didn't think there was anything wrong with her. She needed to know the truth, but did she need to know it all right now?

"I have to tell you," I said, "I'm very worried indeed." I told her I would make another appointment, that I needed to see her again. "There is a problem with her motor responses," I added, knowing that the mother would have no idea what this meant. "She is going to need some physiotherapy."

She looked at me with a penetrating gaze for a few moments. "What exactly are you saying?" she asked.

"What exactly I'm saying," I repeated, "is that she has a problem with her motor responses and she's going to need some physiotherapy."

"Ok." The mother took the appointment card I held out to her and rose to go. I was pretty certain by the time she came back she would have been to the library, looked up motor responses, and figured out for herself that her baby had severe cerebral palsy . There is just no easy way to say this to a parent. I could only hope I had handled it right.

(This is a true story, and I was the mother. I can recall the conversation vivdly, but I decided to try and imagine it from the doctor's viewpoint.)

17. Lawn Mowing and the Presence of God

Last weekend I was cutting my grass between showers. Because it had been raining, the grass was damp, and soon after I had finished it began to rain again. The smell from the newly-mown grass was wonderful, all the more so because of the rain, and it reminded me of the verse that says, "He shall come down like rain upon the mown grass: as showers that water the earth." (Psalm 72.6).

It set me thinking. When the rain falls and waters the earth it brings a lovely, earthy scent with it. When it falls on newly mown grass, the scent has an extra sweetness and richness about it. The presence of God, which is often symbolised in Scripture by rain, always brings refreshing and newness of life. But when we have been through harrowing experiences and feel as if we have been mown down, somehow the sweetness of the rain of God's Spirit in our lives is all the greater.

Sometimes the rain naturally falls and waters everything. At such times, gardening is effortless! But at other times we have to seek out a source to give the land the water it needs. I have an outside tap which I seldom use because my rain-butt collects most of the water I need for my garden. But either way, I have to get out there and water it myself. I have to carry my watering can to where the water is, and then bring it back to the plants.

Of course God is omnipresent; there is never a moment when I'm not in His presence. But somehow He doesn't always seem immanent. Sometimes that's my own fault – the result of neglecting fellowship with Him. At other times, maybe He withdraws His felt presence so that I will seek Him with a new urgency. There are times when the sense of His presence just pours into my life unbidden. And there are other times when I have to go and put myself in the place where the water is, so to speak – to sit by the well; to find where the waterfall is and stand in the spray.

This coming week I'm going to do just that. I'm off to shut myself away to write the second draft of a book I wrote between September and April. But I know that my first need is to seek out God's presence and gaze at Him, allowing His presence to transform me into His likeness. Until I do that, I have nothing worthwhile to write.

18. Nor can foot feel, being shod

The world is charged with the grandeur of God.
It will flame out, like shining from shook foil;
It gathers to a greatness, like the ooze of oil
Crushed. Why do men then now not reck his rod?
Generations have trod, have trod, have trod;
And all is seared with trade; bleared, smeared with
toil;
And wears man's smudge and shares man's smell:
the soil
Is bare now, nor can foot feel, being shod.

And for all this, nature is never spent;
There lives the dearest freshness deep down things;
And though the last lights off the black West went
Oh, morning, at the brown brink eastward, springs—
Because the Holy Ghost over the bent
World broods with warm breast and with ah! bright
wings.

(Gerard Manley Hopkins)

I have just had the privilege of stepping out of
my usual world for four days and spending the time
writing in a lovely old house with an enchanting
garden. All around me, and quite undaunted by my
presence, have been collared doves, dunnocks, jays,
magpies, blackbirds, thrushes and a green
woodpecker which fluttered between the trees and
even, on one occasion, sat on the ground less than
two feet from me, making its characteristic laugh.

I have had time to notice the buttercups and
speedwells in the grass, the stunningly gorgeous
waterlilies now fully open in the pond, the delicious
scent of the dew-covered lawn first thing in the

morning, the soft caress of the blades of grass between my toes and the musical trickle of the fountain in the centre of the pond. Coupled with the excellent meals that have appeared in front of me three times a day, all of my senses have been fully engaged in the present moment, in a feast of appreciation of the wonderful world God has placed me in.

It has made me think..... how often I surround myself with a hard layer of busyness that keeps me from feeling the full effect of all that is around me. I am in exceptionally beautiful surroundings here, but there is no shortage of beauty in my own home; the problem is that I cushion myself against its impact and so often the present moment passes me by as I bury myself in activity or withdraw into emotional numbness to avoid painful memory. It is as if my soul's foot, being shod, can no longer feel.

Taking off the shoes is always an action of great significance in the Bible. The classic example we always think of is Moses removing his shoes before the burning bush, only to find himself in the presence of the God previously unknown to him, whose name is I Am. Often on a Sunday morning when I'm in the middle of the congregation of the family of God, I slip out of my shoes; it is a gesture that has significance for me as a mark of my reverence towards God.

But there are other Biblical examples, too. Boaz's relative removed a shoe as part of the ceremony which established Boaz's status as Ruth's Kinsman-Redeemer, and his willingness to become her husband. Maybe I'm stretching the analogy a little, because it was the relative, not Boaz, who removed the shoe. But bear with me, because here's a thought. God has removed His shoes. When Jesus hung on the cross, the nails were driven through His unshod feet. It was His sign that He was making Himself not only our Redeemer but our Kinsman too, and securing Himself a Bride for all eternity.

When I return home shortly, I am resolving to spend more time barefoot in my garden, feeling the grass between my toes and being deliberately conscious of the sacrament of the present moment, the presence of God in tangible reality within me and around me. I am also resolving to keep my soul unshod, to stop protecting it and allow its vulnerability to be both a channel through which I can feel and experience the Spirit of God present in me and a sign of my desire to revere and honour God in my everyday life.

19. Samuel Rutherford

What a pity that so much pastoral correspondence now takes place through texts, emails, phonecalls, and won't be preserved for the encouragement of future generations!

When life gets tough, I often find myself turning to the letters of Samuel Rutherford. No matter what difficulties I may be facing, they pale into insignificance beside all that he went through. Yet he learned to trust adversity and make a friend of it, because every trial he went through served only to make him lean all the harder on Jesus, and there he always discovered some new facet of His glory which made all the suffering worthwhile.

He was born in 1600, and as a very small child he fell into a deep well. The children he was playing with ran to fetch his father, who arrived to find little Samuel sitting dripping on the side of the well. He told his father that "a bonny white man came and drew me out". A very bright scholar, Rutherford graduated with a master's degree at the age of 21, and at 24 he first surrendered his life to Jesus.

During his lifetime he endured much sorrow. His 2 little children died, and then his wife died also after a painful illness and many nights of torment which Rutherford could hardly bear to watch. All this made him a very tender and loving pastor who understood the troubles that his people faced. He became minister of the small Scottish parish of Anwoth, and as a truly Christlike pastor he had a deep love for his flock. He was unafraid to speak out against political wrongs in the nation or heresies in the national church, resulting in his exile to Aberdeen and ban from preaching. This was a source of almost unbearable grief to him. Since the death of his wife and children, caring for his beloved flock and preaching Christ to them had been his one great joy. Of this time he wrote "Next to Christ I had but one joy, the apple of the eye of my delights, to preach Christ my Lord; and they have violently plucked that away from me."

During his banishment he at first struggled with dejection and a sense of abandonment; and yet as time passed he began to discover that in his isolation he could enjoy the most wonderful "love-feasts" with the One whom he sometimes referred to in his letters as his "only, only Lord Jesus". His great love for his congregation at Anwoth led him to fear that during his absence wolves would come in among his flock. And so he wrote them letters to encourage them in the Lord. Two centuries later some 200 of these letters were collected together and published by Andrew Bonar.

Lady Kenmure was one of his parishioners, and she and her husband were very dear to him. She lost three little daughters in early infancy – a sorrow which he could well understand from his own experiences. When she was 7 months pregnant with a son, her husband also died, and finally the boy died at the age of four, leaving her alone in the world. Rutherford was astonished that God had allowed this last, greatest sorrow to befall her, and he wrote to her with the utmost empathy and tenderness, acknowledging that her grief "will have its own violent incursions in your soul: and I think it will not be in your power to help it." But he also wrote these words, which have carried many a suffering Christian through earthly hardships – and I count myself among them: "I shall believe for my part that He mindeth to distil heaven out of this loss, and all others the like; for wisdom devised it, and love laid it on, and Christ owneth it as His own, and putteth your shoulder beneath only a piece of it."

Eventually Rutherford was able to return to Anwoth, but he was only there a year before the church authorities appointed him professor of divinity at St Andrews and once again he had to leave Anwoth. He continued to write his letters from there.

To a dying man who had lived a worldly life and was afraid of death, he wrote these words: "I find this world, when I have looked upon it on both sides, within and without, and when I have seen even the laughing and lovely side of it, to be but a fool's idol, a clay prison....I recommend Christ and His love to you, let Him have the flower of your heart."

Eventually Rutherford remarried, and over time he and his wife buried 6 of their 7 children in infancy. Even then he could write, "Why should I start at the plough of my Lord, that maketh deep furrows on my soul? I know that He is no idle husbandman, He purposeth a crop." The secret of this confidence, this ability to hold fast to his faith in God through the hardest of trials, stemmed from the intimacy with Jesus which he had learned to cultivate during his time of exile.

I think this is why I so often turn to Rutherford in difficult times; it's not that he is simply a role model, nor that his words are comforting; he's not a leaning post but a signpost, pointing me always to Jesus, the true Comforter: "There are curtains to be drawn by in Christ, that we never saw, and new foldings of love in Him. I despair that ever I shall win to the far end of that love, there are so many plies in it....His love surroundeth and surchargeth me. I am burdened with it; but oh, how sweet and lovely is that burden!" "Oh, what a fair One, what an only One, what an excellent, lovely, ravishing One, is Jesus! Put the beauty of ten thousand thousand worlds of paradises, like the Garden of Eden, in one....And yet it would be less to me than that fair and dearest well-beloved, Christ." Of his sufferings he wrote, "O sweet, sweet is His yoke! Christ's chains are of pure gold; sufferings for Him are perfumed. I would not give my weeping for the laughing of all fourteen prelates; I would not exchange my sadness with the world's joy. O lovely, lovely Jesus, how sweet must Thy kisses be, when Thy cross smelleth so sweetly!"

Finally, Rutherford lay on his deathbed, calling for a harp to join in with the music of heaven which he could already hear. His wife had died before him, and at his side was his 1 precious remaining child, an 11 year old girl named Agnes, who was about to be orphaned by his death. But he knew that the Jesus who had brought him through all the storms of life would also take care of her, and so he simply said, "I have left her upon the Lord."

Ultimately, the hope that sustained him was the same hope that we share, but we're almost 400 years closer to it than he was: "Christ will be upon us in haste; watch but a little, and ere long the skies will rive and that fair lovely person, Jesus, shall come in the clouds, freighted and loaded with glory."

20. A Multitude of Tender Mercies

"Have mercy upon me, O God, according to Thy lovingkindness: according to the multitude of Thy tender mercies, blot out my transgressions. Wash me throughly from mine iniquity, and cleanse me from my sin." (Psalm 51.1-2)

I seldom read the King James Version. While the English Lit graduate in me revels in the solemn beauty of the cadences in the same way as I would revel in a passage of, say, Shakespeare or Milton, couching all my thoughts about God in 17th century language serves only to make Him feel like a religious object, removed from daily life, rather than my dear and familiar Father. But when it comes to Psalm 51, I do like the KJV. I want a God who is merciful according to His lovingkindness, and who has a multitude of tender mercies for me. Not just great mercy or abundant mercy, but a multitude of tender mercies. The Father who, in the words of Psalm 103, pities me as a father pities his children, because He knows my frame and remembers that I am dust. A God who doesn't beat me up the way I beat myself up, because He is so thoroughly conversant with my frailties, and has so much more patience and compassion with them than I do. A God whose whole heart towards me is tenderness. (To quote Frederick William Faber, "There is no place where earth's sorrows are more felt than up in heaven; there is no place where earth's failings have such kindly judgment given.")

The KJV sounds much deeper and more moving than some of the modern versions (NLT: "Have mercy on me, O God, because of your unfailing love. Because of your great compassion, blot out the stain of my sins." GNB: "Be merciful to me, O God, because of your constant love. Because of your great mercy wipe away my sins!" The Message: "Generous in love — God, give grace! Huge in mercy — wipe out my bad record. Scrub away my guilt, soak out my sins in your laundry.") All due respect to the translators/paraphrasers but to me this just doesn't do justice to the sentiments or carry the same force. And that delicious word "throughly" somehow conjures up a much more vivid picture than the modern equivalent, "thoroughly" – "throughly" sounds somehow more efficaciously penetrating than "thoroughly".

And I particularly want God to be merciful. I want Him to have a multitude of tender mercies towards me; that sounds like exactly the balm my soul is in need of. I want to be cleansed throughly from my sins, not just thoroughly but throughly, no half measures; I just want to be shot of the whole lot, to feel the entire burden fall from me like Bunyan's Pilgrim at the cross. But I can't be the child of a Father who lavishes a multitude of tender mercies on me unless I'm also prepared to do the same for those who've offended me. And there's the rub. As I come face to face with one who has wronged me, can I find in my heart a multitude of tender mercies? Can I blot out their transgression according to the measure of lovingkindness that God has lavished on me?

The answer ought to be yes. Last February I had a magazine article published on forgiveness. Several people wrote to me and to the magazine to say it had been helpful. So to find myself struggling with feelings of unforgiveness feels at best embarrassing, at worst hypocritical. Worse still, Jesus was clear that God forgives in the way and to the extent that we forgive others. I don't want a measly, grudging let-off from God. I want that multitude of tender mercies, the cleansing "throughly" from my sins. So Psalm 51 is a good starting place for me. For my unforgiveness and resentment is as much an offence, in need of forgiveness and cleansing, as any offence done to me. So humbling myself to seek mercy and forgiveness is a good place to start, and I know my Father will give it freely, if He knows that I intend to pass it on – and I do, so help me God.

21. Are you a bishop?

A recent conversation around a cafe table set me thinking. Someone said, "There's a real lack of pastoral care in this church. If it wasn't for such-and-such-a-friend I would have left the church by now." And I found myself thinking, "How is that a complaint about lack of pastoral care? It sounds great to me, as if the members of the body are functioning just as they're meant to do."

In Hebrews 12.15 it says "See to it that no one falls short of the grace of God." The Greek word translated "See to it" is the word ἐπισκοπουντες (episkopountes). Literally it means to have oversight of, or care for, something or someone. This verb derives from the noun ἐπισκοπος (episkopos) which is usually translated in our English Bibles as either overseer or bishop. In other words the writer to the Hebrews (who was it? I like the theory that suggests Priscilla as the author!) is saying oversee each other, look out for one another, exercise the care of a bishop over the flock, to ensure that nobody misses the grace that God has for them.

The interesting thing to note is that this command (because that's what it is) doesn't occur in one of the pastoral epistles. This is not Paul writing to a young pastor encouraging him on how to lead the church. This is written to the ordinary man and woman in the pew. Look, says the Holy Spirit via whoever this author is, all of you should be acting like bishops. A bishop carries as a symbol of his office a shepherd's crook. This is an implement which can assist in crossing rugged or treacherous terrain in search of the lost sheep, and it can be used to reach into inaccessible places to hook the lamb out of peril and back into safety. That, says the writer to the

Hebrews, is the kind of ministry that all of you should be exercising in respect of each other.

So when someone says, "If it wasn't for you I would have left the church", that isn't an indictment of the lack of pastoral care. It's a healthy sign that someone in the congregation understands that he stands in the role of bishop to his fellow members, and has a role in keeping them in the path God has for them, guarding them from straying into a place where they miss out on all God wants to give them. It's not something that is supposed to be left to the pastor, it's a normal part of our role as members of the church of Jesus Christ. Did you know you were a bishop? Who are you overseeing? As long as we're all functioning as we should and looking out for each other, no one will slip through the "pastoral care" net and the body of Christ will be in a healthy state!

22. The Wrath of God

I recently observed a discussion on the subject of the wrath of God. It was sparked by the hymn "In Christ alone" – some parties to the discussion objected strongly to the lines, "And on the cross as Jesus died, the wrath of God was satisfied", one person describing it as "bad theology". I was uncomfortable with the discussion, but for reasons I couldn't entirely put into words, and so I simply observed and didn't participate. Ever since, I have been thinking about why it made me so uncomfortable.

The nearest I could put it into words was that there are some things that make me very angry – things in the world around me, things in society and even in myself. I sincerely hope they make God angry, too – otherwise the idea that He is holy, or even minimally just, is meaningless. If I thought God could look at the victims of Jimmy Savile's vile predation and then contemplate Savile's behaviour with benign indulgence, I would be outraged. If I thought he could observe without rage the senseless and wanton destruction of precious human lives in Syria, I would never pray again. I want a God who sometimes feels wrath. But this in itself did not fully explain my unease at the discussion – I doubt whether any of the participants would disagree with me this far.

While researching this article, I came across another blog (http://troyhochstetler.wordpress.com/2008/07/07/if-i-could-change-the-lyrics/) which also quoted this hymn and proposed, as an alternative wording, "the love of God exemplified". This, for me, raised more questions than it answered. If the cross is an atonement, it must be the way in which the sin which, I hope, angers God in this world, is dealt with. Otherwise, it isn't an atonement. And if we don't see the cross of Jesus in terms of atonement, it leaves us with a problematic view of God's character.

Firstly, how can sin be forgiven, removed, done away, without being atoned for? Imagine a judge who smiled on and pardoned every offender without ever demanding that they pay for their crimes in some way, or provide some kind of justice for their victims. We wouldn't see such a judge as loving and good so much as unjust and lazy.

Secondly, if the cross was not an atonement which satisfied the wrath of God against human sin, if it was simply God's love exemplified, if God could forgive us without requiring that kind of atonement, then it might have been very nice of Him to identify in this way with our human plight, but it wasn't strictly necessary. And we would have to have very disturbing doubts about a father who allowed his son to suffer the things that Jesus suffered if it wasn't strictly necessary. Surely if there had been any other way at all for our sin to be removed and for us to be reconciled to God, He would have taken it?

These are the implications that we have to think about when we want to remove the idea of the wrath of God. Please don't misunderstand me. I don't believe God is judgemental, even though I believe He is a righteous judge. I don't believe God is a God of punishment, even though I believe justice demands that sin is punished. I believe that God is actively looking for opportunities to shower His grace on us, that He is not willing that any should perish, and that there will be vastly fewer people in hell than the average evangelical upbringing might lead you to expect.

I think that, paradoxically, God is far more aware than we are of the enormity and vileness of our sin, those little character traits which we're not proud of, which we try to explain away as the result of tiredness or stress; and yet he takes a far more kindly and understanding view than we do of our failings, does not condemn us when we condemn ourselves, knows our frame and remembers that we are dust.

Since the discussion was a few weeks ago, why am I blogging about it now? I have just been to the funeral of a much-loved aunt, taken from us too soon. She had anticipated her death, though I don't think she realised how soon or how suddenly it would come, and had planned her own funeral, including hymns and Bible readings. She had chosen the offending hymn which started the discussion. She had also chosen "Before the throne of God above". She had exemplified the calm trust with which a lover of Jesus, who knows herself also to be His beloved, slips gently into His direct presence without fear or doubt. Letter upon letter had been received by her family from neighbours who had been on the receiving end of her kindness and practical help.

As I thought about the example of her life and her death, and with the words of scripture and hymns still ringing in my ears from her funeral, I began to see afresh the wonder of exactly what Jesus accomplished for us by His death. I stood in a crowded place today, looking at a sea of faces, people who, by and large, are probably unaware of God's tender heart of compassion for them, unaware of the way in which their own sinfulness places a barrier between them and Him, unaware that He did the only thing He could to sweep that barrier away and sacrificed His own Son in an atoning death that dealt with all that keeps them away from Him.

I wanted to stand up and sing at the top of my lungs,
"Because the sinless Saviour died,
My sinful soul is counted free,
For God the just is satisfied
To look on Him and pardon me."

Instead I prayed that God will send such an outpouring of the Holy Spirit that hearts all over this nation, indeed this world, will open to His love and forgiveness. And I resolved to lose no opportunity to share His love with those who come within my reach every day – neighbours, friends, Big Issue sellers, and anyone else whom He sends my way.

23. In Naaman's Footsteps

3 weeks ago I did something rather strange, following in the footsteps of someone else who had done the same thing a few weeks earlier. Like Naaman in 2 Kings 5, I was dipped 7 times, only not in the river Jordan, but the bapstistry of the King's Centre, Aldershot. I had listened to Jan's testimony after her 7-fold dipping, and several parts of it had spoken to me, including a passage she read about the undragoning of Eustace from The Voyage of the Dawn Treader by C S Lewis, which closely mirrored something God was already saying to me.

However, I didn't immediately sign up to follow suit, mainly because I didn't want to jump on the latest bandwagon, but only to hear from God and follow His direction. Over the next couple of weeks, I actively spent time asking God if this was something He wanted to use in my life as He clearly had in Jan's.

Then I had a counselling session in which I was asked to describe how I saw my journey, the future that I'm now facing post-divorce. I felt as if I had let go of the future I thought I was going to have and which I wanted all along, in which God would redeem our marriage and we would have a future together which was radically different from our past. That didn't happen, and I had to let go of that, and instead there was a doorway into another future, very different from the one I thought I was going to have, but very good nonetheless. But I felt as if, instead of going through that doorway, I had fallen into a black hole somewhere between the two. As we allowed the Holy Spirit to explore that with us, I had a picture of myself standing outside that doorway to the new future, and it wasn't that I had fallen down a black hole, it was that I was still carrying so much baggage on my back that I just couldn't fit through the doorway. I went through a process of naming the things I was still carrying and putting them down, and then went through the doorway. I closed that door on everything I had put down, and asked Jesus to lock it so that no one could open it again.

At once I knew that this Naaman-like dipping was the next step. It was not a baptism – I had been baptised into the Body of Christ as a teenager, and God has honoured that, as He always does. This was not a case of being re-baptised. The thing that spoke to me about Naaman's story was that Naaman emerged with his skin made new like that of a little child, and God was speaking to me about the need for me to go through a process of casting off all the adult stuff that has made me hard and cynical and become childlike again, rediscovering an innocent simplicity in my walk with Him.

Some changes we become aware of immediately; others emerge over time as the result of a process. Immediately after the dipping I knew the Holy Spirit had done something in me, sealing what had happened earlier when the door was closed on everything that had been holding me back. I experienced an immediate release in prayer, a new freedom to come to my Father in that childlike simplicity I had been longing for. I felt like a baby just starting out with everything to learn.

False images of God which I had struggled with fell away as He revealed to me afresh His tender heart of compassion, and the loveliness of Jesus. Habits and temptations which had kept me from Him, or behind which I had been hiding, were broken. These things I knew immediately.

One other thing has emerged over the three weeks since then. I had every expectation that this event was going to change me and affect my future. If I hadn't had that faith, I wouldn't have bothered going through with it. But what has surprised me is that it has also changed the way I view my past. Things that previously were just painful memories have taken on a different aspect. The adventure I thought I was setting out on didn't materialise, but I have been on a very different adventure instead. It has made me the person I am today, and who knows where it will lead me in the future?

How exciting! And what an amazing God we serve, endlessly creative in His ways of reaching and changing us, infinitely capable of surprising us and doing exceedingly abundantly above all that we can ask or even dream of.

24. Some musings on Christmas and old age

I've spent part of every week since September caring for my mum who is becoming quite frail, and for my aunt who, although older than my mum, has been caring for her for the past few years to the point of exhaustion. The weeks I've spent with them have confirmed some things we all know about old age – it is a time of memories, frailty, increasing dependence. But there are some things about it that have been new observations for me.

I had never really appreciated before that old age is a time of multiple bereavement. In the past 3 years my mother has probably lost around a dozen close friends and family each year. She feels the loss as keenly as any younger person would do. Her much loved sister-in-law died last month, and I have learned today of the death of another treasured aunt.

I've been impressed with what a large proportion of each day my mum and her sister spend in prayer – whether alone, together, or corporately in church. They are clearly deepening their relationship with the One they long to see face to face at last.

And my mother exposes the truth about that wicked lie put forward by the euthanasia lobby – that increasing dependence on others for personal care involves a loss of dignity that is worse than death. I have seen very clearly that loss of dignity is an interior state of mind, one that my mother refuses to entertain – she accepts my ministrations with a poise, grace and dignity that come from within.

Thinking all this over, my mind has travelled to another old lady – Anna. The Greek in Luke 2 is a little ambiguous. Some translations have it that she was married for seven years and then a widow until she was eighty-four. Others suggest that she was married for seven years and then widowed for a further eighty-four. Assuming she married at about thirteen or fourteen as was customary, that would make her about one hundred and four.

Either way, it was a great age for that time. She would have seen almost all of her contemporaries predecease her. We are not told whether she had children – even if she did, life expectancy at the time was such that they might possibly have died before their mother. No employment would have been open to her, and in all probability she had lost everyone who might have been able to support her. She certainly knew what it was to lose loved ones, and to be stripped of everything that mattered until God was all she had left.

Anna spent her days in the temple, worshipping, fasting and praying. In fact, we're told she never left the temple. Like my mother, she had been captivated by the love of a Father who was worth devoting her whole life to, and she eagerly anticipated a face-to-face meeting with her Saviour, even though unlike my mother she didn't know who He was or when He would come. The moment she saw the baby Jesus, she recognised Him because she had spent a lifetime attuning her ear to the Father's voice.

This peasant couple, looking like any other poor and powerless family, unnoticed by most in the temple, caught her attention not because there was something striking about their son's outward appearance but because, like Simeon, she had spent her whole life looking for the Messiah, and the eyes of her heart were wide open so as not to miss His coming.

So even though the whisper in her heart, "Here He is! This is the one who will bring redemption!" was imperceptible to all those around her, she heard it loud and clear. Simeon declared that he was ready to depart in peace, and Anna lifted her voice in thanksgiving to God. I hope that by the time I'm her age I will have spent my life drawing so near to Him that I don't miss His finest whispers or His most scarcely perceptible arrivals.

I pray that all of us who long for His coming – not just His second coming, but His manifest coming in revival in response to many heartfelt prayers, will spend the interim in intimate communion with Him, preparing our hearts so that should He come, as He has in the past, in a guise that many do not recognise, we will be so straining the eyes and ears of our hearts to catch a glimpse and whisper of Him that we will not miss the moment.

"Consider the incredible love that the Father has shown us in allowing us to be called 'children of God'—and that is not just what we are called, but what we are. Our heredity on the Godward side is no mere figure of speech—which explains why the world will no more recognise us than it recognised Christ. Oh, dear children of mine (forgive the affection of an old man!), have you realised it? Here and now we are God's children. We don't know what we shall become in the future. We only know that, if reality were to break through, we should reflect his likeness, for we should see him as he really is! Everyone who has at heart a hope like that keeps himself pure, for he knows how pure Christ is." 1 John 3. 1-3, JB Phillips

25. On Christmas Newsletters

I have now lost count of the number of rants I've heard this year against Christmas newsletters. I read one yesterday suggesting that the portrayals of perfect children make us feel very insecure about our own offspring, and Lynne Truss on Radio 4 has been listing increasingly offensive ripostes which might be sent to discourage the recipient from ever sending another one.

Frankly, I don't get it. There are people who have been pivotal in my life – childhood friends, university friends, former fellow church members, distant cousins, whose paths no longer cross with mine in daily life. We have settled in different parts of the country or the world and the only news we hear of each other is via the Christmas newsletter.

I can't imagine the curmudgeonly spirit that finds these missives annoying. Of course they contain only the edited highlights. Well, most of them. I have one friend whose annual letter is a catalogue of woes – ailments, disputes, accidents. The nadir was the year she described the boils on her 20-year old son's bottom and the measures she was having to take to dress them. But this is the exception. Most people know how much information is too much.

Because I haven't seen many of these friends over the years, in most cases I've never met their children. But I've followed their stories, annual episode by annual episode, with genuine interest. I think people are wonderful creatures. I love to hear about them. I welcome the chance to rejoice in someone's success, even someone I've never met. I love that even if a son or daughter hasn't turned out to be an academic high flyer or an amazing career genius, a parent's love can still single out things about their life to celebrate.

Most of these children and young adults I wouldn't recognise if I passed them in the street. But that doesn't stop me taking a real interest in what they're doing. C.S. Lewis once said, "There are no 'ordinary' people. You have never talked to a mere mortal." He was right. Every human person is an eternal soul with a streak of pure genius in some area of life. I recently met up with some distant cousins at a family funeral. Some of their children I haven't met since they were very small, some I had never met before. They are all doing amazing things with their lives – a book illustrator, an events organiser, a mother of four, and one is the director of Action for Happiness. Thanks to Christmas newsletters I already knew what they were all doing, and that greatly enhanced my experience of meeting them at last and being able to put faces to the names.

People are wonderful, amazing creatures. The humblest and most obscure of them achieves so much. Even my disabled daughter whose life and possibilities are so limited has a zest for life that many a self-important business executive should envy. I hope that when people read my annual letter they enjoy reading about my children too. Imagine that mother of four. She is raising responsible, caring citizens who will contribute who knows what to this world in the future. How exciting! So please, keep your newsletters coming. I look forward to receiving them, I promise you I read every one, I love to hear your news and they remind me to pray for your families.

26. The undeserving, the scroungers, the abusers…. A worthy cause?

Your mission is to the undeserving – the scroungers who could help themselves if they weren't so lazy, the illegals who shouldn't even be here, the perpetrators of abuse, the ones who know what they're doing is wrong but find it easier to continue than to try to stop. Your task is to bless them beyond their wildest dreams and certainly way, way beyond anything they deserve. Would you accept the mission? Can you imagine what the Daily Mail would have to say?

This is what Easter is about – this was Jesus' mission.

The scrounger who found it easier to live off other people (Zacchaeus) found something far greater than material wealth – forgiveness, acceptance, generosity and restoration to his community.

The illegals who shouldn't even be in the community in the first place – the lepers who were supposed to stay outside the town where they couldn't contaminate anyone – they weren't ordered out of town, they were touched by a gentle, fearless hand, healed and restored to God and man.

The perpetrators of abuse – those men who dragged a woman from her lover's bed (leaving him unscathed, of course), hauled her naked and shamefaced through the street without stopping to enquire what kind of abuse made her flee her husband in the first place – they were given a chance to find within themselves a place of humility and compassion which opened a door to living differently in future, a gesture that made real change possible.

And the one who knew what he was doing was wrong, but found it easier to continue – Pilate, the man who knew even as he washed his hands of the whole affair that he'd had the chance to save the life of an innocent man and had chosen not to – he too was encompassed in that "Father, forgive them, they know not what they do."

And me. The one who would sometimes rather nurse a comforting grievance than walk the costly path of forgiveness. The one who, from the security of marriage, used to look down on those whose sexual mores didn't conform to Biblical norms – until the marriage failed and I found myself a single mum on benefits. I will admit that changed my perspective. The one who is so often more concerned with being right than with admitting my imperfection and my need of grace. His mission was to me, too.

It's a bitter pill to swallow at first – that God cares as much about the burglar who ransacked your home, the abuser who stole your innocence, the drug dealer lurking outside your local school, the drunk driver who killed your precious child, as he does about you.

But it's also a glorious draught of freedom. Because if God's love does not encompass all of humanity, there's a possibility that I could do something that puts myself beyond its scope. As it is, I know that nothing, nothing I will ever do, no secret I carefully buried in the past, no scornful abuser making me feel less than nothing, no stinking pride and superiority making me feel better than everyone, no grinding poverty and no choking wealth will ever put me beyond the scope of the love of God. That was Jesus' mission, and with His cry of "It is finished!" He was announcing, "Mission accomplished."

27. "Before I was afflicted I went astray, but now I obey Your commands" (Psalm 119. 67)

I remember once reading a book, and I'm going to have to be very imprecise about the attribution here, but I think it was probably one by Jamie Buckingham. He described meeting an elderly man who had a particularly close relationship with God. He asked the man how he had come to know God so intimately, and received the reply, "How does anyone come to know him? Trouble!"

I was thinking about that this morning as I was taking stock of my own journey. I don't claim to be close to God in the way that man was, but I do recognise that my journey has been bringing me closer to Him.

There has been "trouble" in my life. There is "trouble" going on now. In all of that, God hasn't changed, but my responses both to Him and to "trouble" have changed.

As a teenager, I went through a very traumatic incident. The disturbance it caused built up in me for a couple of years, years during which I discovered the French Existentialists. By the time I had immersed myself thoroughly in their philosophy, I could see no point in going on, and made several suicide attempts.

After that, I found my way back to faith in Jesus by a rather intellectual route and settled into a somewhat cerebral relationship with Him that had little effect on my everyday life, though it did give me a taste for apologetics – that's probably why I eventually ended up teaching religion, philosophy and ethics.

During that time I made a disastrous marriage, and began to make the first tentative steps towards finding God for myself. Like Leah in the Old

Testament, I craved my husband's love and dedicated a lot of time to trying to win it, and like Leah I gradually came to a place where I resigned myself to the status quo and praised God instead (see Genesis 29.35). I was beginning to form a very vague idea that my affirmation and self-worth could never come from any other human and would have to come from God. The trouble was, at that stage I had only the vaguest idea what God was like, and He was more to be feared than approached.

Four years into the marriage I gave birth to a very seriously disabled child. For 3 months she fought for life in hospital, and when she eventually came home it took two and a half hours to feed her, which had to be done six times a day, so fifteen hours out of every twenty-four were spent trying to feed her. Even so she failed to thrive and at five months old weighed only four pounds and fourteen ounces. In addition, she stopped breathing six or eight times in every twenty-four hours and I had to rush to her again and again, day and night, to restart her breathing. Sometimes she wouldn't start, or only very inadequately and we had to make an emergency dash to hospital. During her first two years of life she was in hospital twenty-four times with pneumonia, her lungs damaged by ten weeks on a ventilator.

At fifteen months old, she was diagnosed with quadriplegic cerebral palsy and a learning disability, which subsequently turned out to be severe autism. God seemed to be a million miles away. If He knew what we were going through, He didn't seem to care. This fearful, distant God whom I had decided to follow appeared to be quite absent in my hour of need. But then a friend's testimony of how tragedy had drawn him very close to God caught my attention. I cried out to God that I didn't care what I had to go through, I just wanted to reach that place of abundance which my friend had described. Things got dramatically worse as my baby became still sicker. But God intervened in a dramatic way (the story is too long to tell here). I began to realise that He did know what I was going through, and He did care enough to get involved.

Shortly after this, my life was quite literally turned around by coming across this verse in the Psalms: "Listen O daughter, consider and give ear; forget your people and your father's house. The King is enthralled by your beauty. Honour Him, for He is your Lord." (Psalm 45. 10-11). My false ideas of God were overturned in a moment. I saw that He delights in me and longs that I will feel the same way about Him.

Thus began a love affair that became the wellspring of my life. It carried me through another 27 years of painful marriage. I can't pretend I have been as faithful to God as He has been to me. Shortly before my eventual divorce I remember quoting Shakespeare's words to my pastor: "As flies to wanton boys are we to the gods; they kill us for their sport." But such cynicism couldn't last in the face of God's relentless love. As my marriage entered its death throes I came to appreciate and rely on His unfailing faithfulness.

The day I moved into my own home as a newly single woman, I didn't even feel as if I was single, because I had such a strong sense of God moving in with me as my Husband. That's why I haven't rushed out to join dating agencies or look for someone new – Jesus is all I need, His love is sufficient for me.

There is still trouble going on – one of my daughters is seriously ill; one is having a crisis in her university course; my disabled daughter, now quadriplegic, partially sighted and with a profound learning disability is experiencing a lot of pain and all the while the DWP are trying to assess her as fit for work – a battle I could rather do without at present! I'm caring for my elderly mother, too. But one thing has changed along the way.

Never, even for a moment, do I doubt God's love or blame Him for my hardships. Through it all, by an imperceptibly gradual process, He has drawn really close to me and poured His love into my heart. It has become a well that never runs dry; no matter what demands life is making of me I can always be replenished from that unending supply. Maybe by the time I'm as old as the man in Jamie Buckingham's story, I will exude that same closeness and intimacy with God – I really hope so.

One thing I do know. None of this has happened because I've been a particularly good Christian, or have been exceptionally faithful to God. Quite the reverse. I've had my moments, my doubts, my wobbles, even my times of open rebellion. But God's love has been unswervingly faithful. He is the Rock I can rely on no matter what in my life falls apart. I really love Psalm 91.4: "His faithfulness will be your shield and rampart." Yes. It's His faithfulness, not mine, that has got me this far. All the pressure is taken off me when I realise that it depends on His faithfulness, not mine. Mine will wobble and shake and evaporate, but His remains rock solid. Trouble? It's not what I would have chosen. But then again, if that's what it took to know His precious, tender, faithful, sustaining love, it's been worth every moment.

28. Luke 8.1-3

He began going around from one city and village to another, proclaiming and preaching the kingdom of God. The twelve were with Him. And we were with Him, too. Who else would have allowed us to travel with them? No other rabbi would even have noticed that we existed, let alone tolerated our presence on a preaching trip.

No other rabbi would drop their pearls of wisdom into the ears of women; without exception they would all consider that on a par with throwing valuable family heirlooms into the Valley of Hinnom. Other women, if they heard any rabbinical teaching at all, it was because their husbands cared to pass it on to them. But most husbands wouldn't have bothered.

But Jesus – he had time for every one of us. He talked to us, He let us listen to His teaching, and He really listened to us – you could point to any one of us in this group and He would immediately be able to tell you her deepest concerns, who she cared about, what were her hopes and dreams. He really knew each one of us, and He didn't treat us as lesser beings just because we were women. I've never met another man like Him.

You can imagine how much we all loved Him. Each of us had her own reasons for loving Him. I had seven reasons to love Him – once upon a time I was possessed by seven demons. They haunted my dreams and tormented my mind. They destroyed my self-respect so that I didn't care who used my body or what they did with it. I thought I deserved it all anyway.

Then I met Jesus. And He turned my life on its head. He took my soul and shook it upside down until every last one of those demons fell out, and then He set me right way up. It was like emerging from a thick fog. I had lived my life in confusion for many years, never knowing what to believe, except that I was ugly and undeserving.

But when He came, I stepped out of the fog into the Light. Suddenly I could see clearly. First I experienced Him as an authoritative Commander. He ordered those demons to go away and leave me alone, and they had no choice but to obey. And once they'd gone, I remember that I stood there, fully clothed, but feeling a bit naked because I could see that He knew exactly what I was – well – not what I was any more, but what I had been. I was half expecting Him to come on to me.

But no – He treated me with immense tenderness, the way a really loving brother treats his sister. The way my own brothers had long ago ceased to treat me. And in that brotherly love that radiated from Him, I began to see myself clearly, not a worthless piece of trash but a jewel of great beauty created by God Himself to enhance the glory of His world. It took my breath away.

No wonder I followed Him. There was nothing I wouldn't do for Him. All those years doing the devil's work, I had managed to salt away a bit of money from my life as a working girl. And suddenly here I was, part of this amazing entourage, and I had something really worthwhile to spend that money on – supporting Him and the work He was doing. I felt as if I'd fleeced hell to fund the Kingdom of heaven.

If you asked me to describe Him, I'd say He was my brother, my shepherd, my rescuer, my Lord. He was the reason I got up in the morning, and He was the reason I didn't go back to my old life. Every time He turned that brotherly smile on me I felt whole. He never undressed me with His eyes; instead He clothed me with a cloak of beauty and priceless worth. Little, humble me – I felt like a royal princess whenever I was near Him.

And as we travelled from place to place I saw Him again and again dive into whatever mess people had got themselves into and pull them out of it. For me He personified the words of the Psalmist when he spoke of God who heard my cry and pulled me out of the pit of destruction, out of the miry clay, set my feet upon a rock, making my footsteps firm, and put a new song in my mouth, a song of praise to our God. The Psalmist described how God did that for him, and that's exactly what Jesus did for me. He's the only God I will ever worship. I'm going to be singing His praises as long as I live, this brotherly, fatherly, kingly man whose love rescued me.

29. The Arrival

I laid my love to rest today. When I say my love, I actually mean my ex-husband, the father of my three daughters. The divorce wasn't of my choosing; in a way it wasn't of his either. It's a complicated story, I won't tell it here. He was a man I feared. He was also the only man I've ever loved, and the divorce didn't change that – I could no longer live with him, but I didn't stop loving him. There's an element of relief that the fear is over; but it is dwarfed by the overwhelming sense of grief. There was an opportunity before he died to speak words of forgiveness and reconciliation. I know that by the end he was at peace with God and we will meet again one day. In trying to find words for my grief and hope, I wrote this poem which I read at the service of thanksgiving for his life:

The Arrival

Your arrival came too soon for me,
So that it seemed no coming, but a leaving;
More like a vessel putting out to sea
Than what it was – the Father's arms receiving
The son his heart had yearned so long to see.

Nothing but the lapping of the waves
Remains, a quiet wake behind your sailing,
And the deep echo in the distant caves,
And the sea-mist, your last departure veiling,
And the sad lapping, lapping of the waves.

But, beyond where mortal eyes can see,
A Father on a distant shore is dancing,
Powerless to contain the ecstasy

At seeing his dear child so close advancing.
I know you rest where you were born to be;
But your arrival came too soon for me.

30. Matthew 11. 25 - 30

One day He came to our city. I had heard so much about Him, and I had often wished I could see and hear Him. That was before the catastrophe struck, the illness that carried my husband away. Maybe if He had been here then, He could have saved him. It was too late now.

But He had come; and the town was in uproar. All the neighbours had packed small loaves and leather bottles of water and gone out for the day to follow Him and hear what He would say. They had not invited me – I was still in mourning, and would not be expected to go.

But if I did not go – what then? I would sit indoors all day with the same thoughts going round in my head, the same old thoughts that had been troubling me for the past week. Thoughts of my three daughters, now almost grown – but where would I get husbands for them without his help? I didn't go about in the community and meet people as he did in his work as a tradesman. Where would I meet suitable families? For one daughter it would be hard enough – but for three? And my poor girls, consumed with grief as they were for their father – how could I help to steer them through their mourning when I hardly knew how to cope with my own grief? And my mother – he had chopped her firewood every day, and dug her field and planted her vegetables. I would have my work cut out managing my own plot; how could I manage my widowed mother's too?

And so that was my choice. Stay at home, as I was expected to, with so many anxieties for company, or creep out and see this young Rabbi that all the world was talking about. Seizing one of the loaves I had just baked, and pouring a little water from the jug into my husband's leather flask, the one he used to take to work, I slipped unseen from my house and made my way to the river's edge where a crowd had gathered. Not being tall, it was quite easy to sneak unnoticed into the back of the crowd at the top of the slope and look down to the waterside, so that I had a good view of the Rabbi without being conspicuous myself.

He was talking, but He wasn't addressing the crowd. His eyes were turned to the skies, and the expression in them almost made it seem as if a light was shining out of His face. I had never seen such pure joy, unmixed with any other emotion except perhaps love for the One He was addressing.

"I praise You Father," He was saying, "Lord of heaven and earth, that you have hidden these things from the wise and intelligent and have revealed them to little children." What things, I wondered. What had He been saying before I got here? I strained to catch His words above the shuffling and fidgeting of the people around me.

"Yes, Father, this is the way that You like best, it pleases You." Then lowering His head, and scanning the crowd before Him as He spoke, he continued, "Everything has been handed over to Me by My Father. No one knows the Son except the Father; nor does anyone know the Father, except the Son, and anyone to whom the Son chooses to reveal Him."

I thought about His words. The one He called the Father – we had never known Him by that name, but we had worshipped Him all our lives; did we not know Him already? But then again, maybe if we really knew Him, we would call Him Father too. I thought of my three daughters. How badly they needed a father! Suppose God could be that Father to them? Suppose He could be a Father to me, too? Then surely He would look after my mother the way my father had done when he was alive.

But how? God was not here, not in any physical way, was He? How could He fill the role of a Father? If only God could come among us! How different things would be. These thoughts were too much for me, they made my head ache under the hot sun. I uncorked my leather flask and drank some water.

My little movement seemed to attract the Rabbi's attention. He turned His gaze in my direction and held it there as He began to speak again, so that He seemed to be speaking directly to me.

"Come to Me, all who are weary and weighed down by heavy burdens, and I will give you rest." He smiled at me, a look of great kindness and empathy. I thought of all the burdens I was carrying – how I would feed myself and my daughters now with no breadwinner, as well as all my other concerns for them and for my mother. Imagine having rest from all that! I couldn't even picture what that would feel like. He continued, first pointing to the field away downstream where a farmer was ploughing with two oxen yoked to the plough.

"Take My yoke upon you and learn from Me," he said. "For I am gentle, and humble in heart, and you will find rest for Your souls." I followed His gaze over to the oxen. The yoke seemed to be an ill fit because they both walked haltingly, stopping intermittently to jerk their heads from side to side, as though the wood chafed their necks.

He seemed to have noticed it too – and noticed me noticing it, because He turned back, picked me out again at the back of the crowd and looked me full in the eye as He said, "My yoke is easy, and my burden is light."

He seemed to be inviting me to yoke myself to Him, to His way of living. There was no doubt, since my husband's death my burdens were heavy. And the way these worries turned themselves around and around in my head all the while, it was exactly like those poor oxen, with something constantly chafing away. Suppose there was a way to be free from all of it?

I sat down on the grass, out of His view, and thought over His words. "Learn from Me," He had said. "I am meek and humble in heart." How? How could I learn that meekness and humility? I thought of the look of joyful trust on His face as He had called God "Father". Surely that was His secret. But then I thought of what else He had said. "Everything has been handed to Me by My Father." Those did not sound to me like words of meekness and humility. They sounded like a very grandiose claim.

Unless…. unless… they were actually true. Then they might just be a matter-of-fact statement. But if so – if He could honestly say, in all meekness and humility, "Everything has been handed to Me by My Father" – what did that say about Him – about who He was? Sitting there in the grass, puzzling it over, it gradually began to dawn on me. What had I wished? If only God could come among us! And here, in this meek and humble young speaker, clad in a simple, homespun robe, with the very light of heaven shining from His eyes, looking at me, right into my soul and seeing all the thoughts and anxieties of my heart – if this was not God come among us, then who else could He be? In all my years of life I had never met another such as He.

And so in the only way I knew how, I learned from Him. I lifted my eyes to heaven in an act of loving trust and whispered the word, "Father." And in that simple act, I felt all the burden of the past days lift from me. The endless chafing of those thoughts stopped, the chatter of the anxieties was silenced. I felt as if I had come home. It was like a child being picked up, wrapped in an embrace and carried to safety. It reminded me of words I had often heard my husband read from the Torah: Underneath are the everlasting arms. I nestled into those arms, and lifted my daughters and my mother to Him, letting go of them into His hands. And as I did so, I was filled with a profound certainty that everything was going to be all right.

31. Dealing with grief (1)

I have just re-read C.S. Lewis's small book, A Grief Observed. I have read it several times before, and it just seemed pertinent reading for me at the moment. Some elements of his experience are, I suppose, pretty universal, except that not everybody would have his outstanding ability to capture it in words.

Other elements I don't identify with. He describes grief as feeling very like fear, and I can't say that has been my experience – at least, not so far. There is a definite sense of it being totally outside my control, but that is already a familiar feeling, having been through a disintegrating marriage and a very unwanted divorce which my most strenuous efforts over many years failed to avert. I have stopped fearing the loss of control, and have become more certain of God's trustworthiness when life is out of control than of any other fact in the universe.

Nonetheless, I am not OK. On Sunday I was willing certain people to ask me how I was. There were a few people present with whom I would have felt safe enough not to wear what my father used to call an "evangeli-grin" and say "fine". There were a few people I wanted to get hold of and say "I am not OK, and I don't know what to do about it." Thankfully one of them did ask me and has kept in regular touch with me all week.

I'm someone who likes my solitude but right now (just as all my closest friends are going away on holiday!) I feel as if I need people around me. Yesterday I wanted to scream at the universe, "I AM NOT ALL RIGHT!"

Today I went down to the sea shore. Not the gently beautiful Mediterranean nor the majestically moving Atlantic, just the sea front at Worthing, the place of my birth. Still, the sea is the sea and I think there can be few ills in life that are not, at least in some degree, cured by a good blustery walk along the sea shore. Sitting there on the shingle I felt the gentle, familiar presence of my Father God, and it was very real. I don't know how anyone can doubt His existence – He manifests Himself so very readily whenever we take time to be still and engage with Him.

And I have come back feeling as if I am not all right, and it's all right not to be all right. But if I am not all right, it is all right. All shall be well, and all shall be well, and all manner of thing shall be well, as Mother Julian said. I feel as if half of me was ripped away when my marriage ended and now that half has gone altogether. Life will never be the same. It may be better, freer, safer – who knows? But it will never be the same. And I am not all right. But I am held by One who has everything in control and who makes no mistakes and who loves me more deeply than I have ever imagined, and at a very fundamental level everything really is all right.

32. Dealing with grief (2)

Two weeks ago I sat on Worthing beach and admitted to God that I am not all right. So what has happened since then? The immediate thing that happened was a profound sense of relief – that it's all right not to be all right sometimes.

The other thing was a deeper sense of engagement with God. I think this is always the result when we are honest with Him. It's not that what we tell Him comes as a startling revelation to Him, of course not – He already knew how I was feeling better than I knew it myself. But somehow being deeply honest with Him about exactly how I am takes down a barrier of my own making and ushers me further into His embrace. It's a good place to be. I would even say, from fairly long experience, it's worth the pain we go through to get to that place.

That was a discovery I first made in 1996 when Ellen had just had major spinal surgery. It saved her life which was by then hanging by a thread. But it also robbed her of some of the scant use she still had left of her limbs and worsened her disabilities. And as her mother I discovered such a depth of comfort in Jesus that I realised it's worth anything we go through just to know that our comfort comes from Him; because if we were never in need of comfort, or never admitted our need, there's a whole aspect of Jesus we would never encounter.

In the past couple of weeks, I have had a bit of a meltdown – I'm still quite fragile, and it doesn't take much to push me into scary-not-coping territory – this week it was something as minor as both our pets being ill that was the final straw.

But, gradually, I am starting to feel, if not all right, then at least that I can see I will at some point be all right again. This is a journey. It can only be taken step-by-step. Flying leaps don't get you further along, they just result in faceplants. Maybe the Psalmist knew that when he wrote, "The steps of a good man (or woman!) are ordered by the Lord, and He delights in his way." Step by step God has marked out this path for me, and as I make each tiny forward movement He is delighted with my progress.

That definitely makes this more bearable because it becomes purposeful. Somehow, somewhere, this experience I am going through fits into God's great scheme of things, and its purpose will one day be revealed. So I am walking through the valley of the shadow of death, not setting up camp here.

33. Dealing with grief (3) Confessions of a bad mother and a bad worshipper

Grief affects the whole family, but affects us all differently. An experience that should draw everyone together, can instead be divisive. I have one ill daughter, one disabled daughter and one neglected daughter at present. I feel I ought to be giving all of them more attention than I am. I also feel I'm so overwhelmed by my own emotions that I haven't any energy left over for handling theirs. As a result we get irritated with each other and tempers fray. Bad mother.

After witnessing a fracas between me and one of my daughters this morning, a friend reminded me that we all need to lean on each other, but no one can do more leaning than weight-bearing, or we all collapse. Wise words. This afternoon I flicked on the radio in time to hear a song with the line, "I worship You and I hide in the shadow of Your wings".

I realised that the reason I'm short on patience with my daughters is that I've allowed my focus to be trained in the wrong direction. It's good to be self-aware, but to be self-analytical is to turn my focus away from Jesus. Instead of worship, which makes me lose myself only to find my true self in Him and Him dwelling in me, I stare at the problems and the feelings, which then loom large.

I love to lie in bed at night with my curtains open, looking up at the night sky, feeling the mystery of having my own place in this vast universe, occupying a slot created just for me. But if that's where it stops, it's not enough; it should lead me into quiet communion with the Maker of it all. And lately, I've neglected that, caught up in my own overwhelming feelings. Bad worshipper.

By the end of this morning, my daughter and I had apologised to each other and I had made a peace-offering cup of coffee! Repairing the minor damage done to that relationship isn't too difficult – just a bit of grace and forgiveness on both sides, and, of course, a hug, because wrapped in someone's arms it's hard to doubt that they love you. She hasn't rejected me as a bad mother!

As for the other relationship – with the One I worship – I ask myself where that has gone wrong, and what needs to be done to put it right. One thing I can identify is that, for many years I was in the habit of getting up early, spending time in prayer, worship and reading the Bible. I journaled my walk with God and my prayer life. It was good from time to time to read back over it, see where I had come from, and marvel at the things God had done in my life. It started out as a real thrill – I gradually woke up earlier and earlier in order to spend more and more time with the One I loved.

But somehow, over time – especially, perhaps, as my marriage was failing, my heart was taking a battering and my ability to trust was being eroded – the very thing that had been an exciting and life-imparting tryst with the Lover of my soul began to become a legalistic ritual, devoid of life and maintained simply because it was something I'd always done and thought I ought to do. There came a point where I strongly felt it was right to stop it and find other, more creative ways of meeting with God. I began to encounter Him more in the ordinary moments of life, just as I had when I first began those early morning meetings with Him.

That was all well and good to start with, but over time I seem once again to have moved from knowing God as my dwelling-place, living all the time in the shadow of His wings, to having Him as my hiding place – I know where to go when trouble hits, but I am increasingly hungry for His presence and longing for the days when He was my constant place of residence. So I am again going to start to get up early and resume those meetings with Him in the quiet before the rest of the household is awake, not because I ought to or it's what I've been taught, but because He says that the way to rekindle our first love is to do the things we did at first – and the memories of those sweet early mornings are still vivid. I shall wrap myself in the prayer-shawl made for me by my friend Cynthia, which itself became for me a symbol of God's presence, and which I haven't used for a while. I'm confident that as I do the first things, the first love will be rekindled.

But crucially, just as my daughters understand that I'm grieving too, and haven't rejected me as a bad mother, God understands more than anyone, more than I do myself, and neither has He rejected me as a bad worshipper. His heart is beautifully expressed in this extract, taken from a hymn which my eldest daughter chose for her father's funeral:

There's a wideness in God's mercy
 Like the wideness of the sea;
 There's a kindness in His justice
 Which is more than liberty.

There is no place where earth's sorrows
 Are more felt than up in Heaven;
 There is no place where earth's failings
 Have such kindly judgment given.

For the love of God is broader
 Than the measure of our mind;

And the heart of the Eternal
Is most wonderfully kind.

But we make His love too narrow
By false limits of our own;
And we magnify His strictness
With a zeal He will not own.

If our love were but more simple
We should take Him at His word,
And our life be filled with glory
From the glory of the Lord.
(Frederick William Faber, 1814 – 1863)

34. Dealing with grief (4)

As a family we are all processing this experience in different ways, some healthier than others. On Sunday afternoon I was doing some gardening and contemplating how each of us is dealing with it. I had a sense of heaviness, and an awareness of a kind of darkness that it was throwing over the family.

In the evening I sat and listened to someone reading Psalm 139. In the middle of this beautiful poem there is a stanza which says:

If I say, "Surely the darkness shall fall on me,"
Even the night shall be light about me;
Indeed, the darkness shall not hide from You,
But the night shines as the day;
The darkness and the light are both alike to You.

And the sense of oppression lifted as I reminded myself that actually, there's no such thing as darkness. What we call darkness is merely the absence of light, the shadow cast by what blocks out the light. I know that God is very present with me – with all of us – in this journey, the God who is light, and in whom there is no darkness at all. And so for a few minutes I sat in silence and revelled in the thought that the darkness and the light are both alike to God; however dark this feels to me, the darkness cannot hide from the God who is light, and therefore the light of God falls even on this darkness, making it shine as bright as the day.

35. A Tale of a Well

Approaching the low wall, I could barely put one foot before the other any longer. We had set out at dawn after a very short night, and the sun was now high and hot in the merciless sky. Every bone ached as I manoeuvred myself down onto the stones and gave a grateful sigh. I was vaguely aware of the others leaving – I supposed in search of food – but I didn't really notice them, or see in which direction they went. My entire attention was occupied by one thing. From my place on the wall I could see right down into the depths of the well, and there at the bottom the cool, shimmering water reflected the sky above me, and mocked my thirst.

The terrible thirst. We had emptied our water flasks long ago, and the sweat had streamed down my face and clothes as I pulled my tired body up the steep mountain paths. I thought back to the dawn of this day, on another mountain many miles away, when I had found a secret spot in the crisp morning to worship and listen. I knew I had to come here, that impression had been unmistakeably clear, but I had no idea why, and looking around me now I saw nothing to give me any clue.

This feeling of searing thirst dominated my whole body and soul and made it hard for me to get my thoughts into any kind of order. I tried to straighten my leaden shoulders and in so doing caught another glimpse of the scornful water far below, winking at my distress. I, always so at one with all things natural, found it more than strange to be at odds with the water that gives life to the earth, but there it was, twenty feet below me, as far out of my reach as if it had been beyond the stars, taunting my parched senses.

A slight scuffling noise caught my attention and I looked to where the path rounded the cliff edge and turned towards the well. A figure shuffled into sight – a woman. Not one of the graceful beauties who come to these wells at dawn and dusk, proud and erect with their water-pots elegantly poised on their stately heads, an easy grace in their gait. This woman was scrambling with effort along the stony path, her head so bowed with care or perhaps shame that she had to clutch at her urn with both hands to keep it on her head.

Consequently, she had almost reached the wall before she looked up and noticed me sitting there. She gave a great start and stepped back a pace, looking at me with a mixture of suspicion and contempt. I took all this in at a glance, but the thing that gripped my attention was the water-pot in her hands.

I struggled to listen to the Spirit of my Father within me – surely now He would show me why I had to come here – it must in some way be connected with this woman. But the screaming thirst made it impossible to think or to hear His still voice in my spirit, and so, without a moment's thought I heard myself blurting out, "Please, will you give me a drink?"

She lowered the pot to the ground, placed her hands on her hips and looked me up and down with one eyebrow raised. I think she could see that I really was gasping and exhausted and something in her womanly soul felt a faint flicker of pity for me. She moved hesitantly towards the well, not taking her eyes off me for a moment.

"You're a Jew," she said, as she tied the rope to the handle of her pot, "and I'm a Samaritan woman. How is it that you ask me for a drink?"

I shrugged. Why did she think I was asking? "Because I'm so thirsty," I responded, nodding towards the urn. "May I have one?"

I watched, moved by the kindness of a stranger as this daughter of Sychar lowered her waterpot with a delicious splash into the cool depths below and began to pull on the rope. She was more beautiful than I had first thought, but her liquid brown eyes and full lips were masked by the expression they wore, a mixture of shame, defiance and fear.

Standing the overflowing pot on the wall beside me, she motioned to me with her hand to help myself and stood watching me, alert with wordless curiosity, as I drank deeply until my thirst was quenched.

"Thank you," I smiled. The well was so deep that even on the hottest of days the water remained cool and refreshing, and I felt myself reviving, both from its hydration, and from the sense that I was here to do my Father's bidding, and that somehow the interaction I was about to have with this woman, however, it developed, was going to be meat and drink to me.

There was a moment of awkward silence, but now it was my turn to be curious, and I voiced my thoughts into the still, stifling air. "It's a strange time of day to be drawing water."

Without blinking she retorted, "It's a strange time of day to be sitting on the wall of that well."

I liked her boldness. "I've come a long journey, and I stopped to rest," I explained. "And you're alone. Have you no friends to come and draw with?"

She shook her head and snorted. "No one wants to associate with me. Nor would you if you knew who I am."

I felt a great surge of love for her from deep within me. It was as if I could see, all at once, who she was made to be and what she had become, and I longed to bridge the gulf between the two. "And if you knew the gift of God," I responded, "and who it is who asks you for a drink, you would have asked him and he would have given you living water."

I wasn't teasing her, certainly not mocking her, and yet she looked at me with so much suspicion, as if she could not see what good motive a man could have for engaging in light-hearted conversation with a woman he'd never met before. At the same time, she was transfixed, unable to turn her gaze away, her curiosity increasing with every word I spoke.

She raised a cynical eyebrow. "Living water, eh?"

I nodded and watched her. There was a hardness and defiance in her voice, but in her eyes the shadow of self-reproach. I longed to hold up a mirror for her to see herself the way my Father saw her.

"Sir," she said, and then abruptly stopped herself. "Well I don't know why I'm calling you Sir," she muttered, more to herself than to me. "It's a long time since I called any man Sir." Then, gathering her thoughts again, "Sir," (she pronounced the word with exaggerated deliberateness) "you have nothing to draw with, and the well is deep. Where are you going to get this living water?"

I made no hurry to reply, but looked thoughtfully at her as I listened to my Father's promptings deep in my spirit.

She threw her shoulders back, tossed her chin up a little and sneered, "Are you greater than our father Jacob who gave us this well and drank from it himself, along with his sons and his livestock?"

I looked at her planted there on the path, so hard and yet so fragile, sweltering under the midday sun, framed by the trees either side, paling the wayside flowers into drabness by her beauty if she did but realise it, so young and so cynical, and felt as if my heart would break.

I picked up her water pot and held it over the path. "If I were to let go of this," I mused, "it would shatter into a thousand pieces. How could you ever gather them up and stick them back together? It would never hold water again."

She reached out and snatched it from me. "Sometimes the soul can feel like that," I continued. "Life has shattered it into pieces. You try to stick them back together, but you can never make it whole again. It will never hold water, and so you have to keep trying to find something to quench the inner thirst."

She was listening now, open-mouthed, her task forgotten. I turned from her and leaned over the well to see the water far below. "Everyone who drinks this water will be thirsty again," I observed. Then I looked back at her, turning so that the well was behind me, spreading out my hands for support on either side of me. "But whoever drinks the water I give them will never thirst."

She gasped audibly. I pretended I hadn't heard and carried on. "In fact the water I give them will become a spring of water inside them, welling up to eternal life." I was willing her to ask more, longing to show her how her thirst for love could be forever quenched in the Father's arms.

I had spoken of pots and I had spoken of souls. What was passing through her mind? I wondered. She turned her eyes away and stared at her water pot.

"Sir," she hesitated, and this time there was no irony in the word, "give me this water so that I won't get thirsty and have to keep coming here to draw water."

Still tuning in to the felt presence of my Father, I debated what subject would draw her out, would come closest to the source of her inner thirst and enable Him to address it. All of a sudden I knew what I had to ask her. "Go, call your husband and come back."

Shock, and then fear registered on her face. I could see her thoughts were racing, trying to decide how to reply. At last she stared at the floor and mumbled, "I have no husband."

And suddenly I could see, behind her, a line of men who had owned and abandoned her, discarded her as worthless, or died taking a chunk of her heart with them, and I knew that her thirst for love went on, so frantic, just as my physical thirst had been when I first sat down here, that she no longer cared how she quenched it.

"You are right when you say you have no husband," I agreed. "The fact is, you have had five husbands, and the man you now have is not YOUR husband. What you have just said is quite true."

She winced at my emphasis on the word "your" and I wondered whose husband it was that she was now living with. The guilt all over her face told me that there was another, wronged, woman involved.

There were tears in her eyes, and a desperation to shift the conversation away from an area so painful. "Sir, she whispered, "I can see that you are a prophet." She waved a hand over in the direction of Gerizim. "Our ancestors worshipped on this mountain, but you Jews say that Jerusalem is the place where we must worship."

I could tell that she hoped the ancient controversy would deflect my thoughts away from her life and all the things she was ashamed of. I looked at this woman, so damaged that she didn't even feel like a woman any longer, and was overwhelmed with an immense tenderness for her, a longing to restore to her all she had been robbed of. "Woman." I chose the word deliberately. "Believe me, a time is coming when you won't worship the Father either on this mountain or in Jerusalem."

Again she gasped, this time at my use of the word "Father". I sat motionless, watching expressions of surprise, curiosity, bitterness and puzzlement pass over her face. After a time she looked back at me again. Seeing I had her attention, I continued.

"You Samaritans worship what you do not know." I was determined to erase the lies and replace them with truth.

"That's true enough."

"We worship what we know. Salvation comes from the Jews."

She tutted and turned contemptuously away. I wanted to bring a reconciliation that transcended any ancient fundamentalism. "But a time is coming – in fact it has now come – when the true worshippers will worship the Father in spirit and in truth, for they are the kind of worshippers the Father seeks."

I had seldom been more conscious of being enveloped in the presence of God. I didn't want to argue theology with her, so I simply held that presence out to her. Her look softened, her defences crumbling.

"I know that Messiah is coming." Her voice was pensive. "When he comes, he will explain everything to us."

I slipped forward and got up from the wall. I walked over until I was standing right in front of her and looked down at her. I know the excitement was shining in my eyes, I couldn't contain it. I looked intently at her. "The one who is speaking with you – I Am."

I saw a moment of incredulity and then a wave of joy engulfed her, transforming that face into the full beauty of its original creation. I knew she had understood. In fact, no further words were needed. She gave a little dance of joy right there on the spot, put down her water pot and ran off into the village, shouting as she ran, "Come and see a man who told me everything I ever did! Could this be the Messiah?"

She ran right past the others as they returned with parcels of food and their refilled water flasks. Peter urged me to eat, but I really wasn't at all hungry and I pushed it away. It was as if my encounter with the woman had filled me right up, I felt replenished. I must have looked it too, because they had left me exhausted on the wall, and here I was standing, energised, as if I had just enjoyed a long and refreshing sleep and a three course meal. The only explanation I could give them was that my nourishment comes from doing what God sent me to do.

As we looked back towards the village, my new friend had gathered a crowd and they were all surging towards us, eager to find out what had happened to her. I turned to the guys who were with me.

"Don't you have a saying, 'It's still four months until harvest'? I'm telling you, open your eyes and look at the fields! They're ripe for harvest." I pointed at the approaching crowd. "Even now the one who reaps draws a wage and harvests a crop for eternal life, so that the sower and the reaper may be glad together.

So the saying 'One sows and another reaps' is true. I sent you to reap what you haven't worked for. Others have done the hard work, and you've reaped the benefits of their labour."

And it was true. That one moment of revelation, that the Father who created her was seeking her, and that in worshipping Him she would find an eternal water-source for her soul, had caused that woman to find a whole harvest-field of other thirsty souls and here they were, ready to be gathered in to the Father who had been seeking them and longing to exchange a heartful of love with them.

36. Another Tale of Another Well

"So, Jesus, if I had been the woman you saw approaching you along that path as you sat, so hot and tired and thirsty on the wall of the well, how would the conversation have gone?"

"I would have asked you for a drink. How would you have responded?"

"I would so much have wanted to give You a drink, enough cool water to fully quench Your thirst. But I would have looked at my vessel and seen, not a large two-handled water-pot, not even a cup, barely a thimble, in fact. And I would have lowered it and scooped up some water and handed it to You, embarrassed at how little I had to offer You."

"And I would have looked at that little offering and seen that though it looked small in your eyes, it was made of pure gold, or to put it another way, true love. And I would have shown you that if you had held it up, you would have seen that, having no base, it was not a thimble but a pipe and that the water flowing through it was infinite."

"And then what?"

"I would have asked you where your husband was. How would you have answered Me?"

"I would have thought it over first. I would have reflected that not only do I have no husband, but I never really had one, that I lost him before the marriage ever really got off the ground, and I lost him again when we divorced, and and I lost him again oh so finally in July. And I would have wondered how to sum that up, and as I thought it over I would have looked at You and suddenly realised that the answer to Your question, where is your husband, is – He is here, You are my true husband, the One whose bride

I am, the One whose love is unfailingly faithful. What would You have said to that?"

"I would have said, as Solomon said to his bride that I have set you as a seal on my heart. And I would have said, as I said to Zerubbabel, that I make you like a signet ring, something that I wear at all times, and there will be no separation, no divorce, no death to part us, and my living water springing eternally up within you will make you fruitful in ways you have never been before."

"And then?"

"And then I stop using the word would, because this is not conditional or hypothetical; this is the way it is from now on."

"I like the picture of the signet ring. When someone is wearing a signet ring, every part of the ring is filled with that person. I like the thought that there's no corner of me that You don't fill. Once that thought would have made me uneasy, but now it seems like the greatest possible security."

"I like it too. Because you think of My love as eternal and so it is, but the unbroken circle of the ring reminds me that your love for Me will never come to an end, either."

This is the conversation I had with the Lord this afternoon. If it has spoken to you in any way, why don't you read through John chapter 4, and then sit down in silence for 20 minutes with no distractions, and ask Jesus the same question I asked Him – "If I had been that woman, how would the conversation have gone?" Write down whatever He whispers to your heart. It might surprise you, reassure you or challenge you. If you are open to whatever He says, you might find it changes your life.

37. Trust the compass

When I was a school teacher, I used to take part in an event every year. Some of our students would complete the Duke of Edinburgh's Award, which included an orienteering task. Students were given a starting point, a finishing point and an Ordnance Survey map. It was up to them how they got from the start to the finish – there were a number of possible routes. Over a few weeks they would study the map, plan their route and list everything they needed to take for a fairly gruelling hike followed by an overnight bivouac.

The staff who organised it put out an annual appeal for teachers to accompany the students on their walk and I usually volunteered and was assigned a group of about 6 students. It was not for me to tell them which route to take, nor to correct their errors. They had to use the map to work these things out for themselves. This was just as well, as I am seriously challenged when it comes to things pictorial. I have a complete mental block about interpreting graphs, diagrams, charts, etc. Map reading is something I find beyond difficult – nearly impossible.

The first time I volunteered for this I learned a very valuable lesson. My little band of students (aged fourteen and fifteen) set out with high hopes and even higher confidence, down the hill on the path they had planned, and deep into the woods. Then things began to get complicated. There were so many more paths between the trees than were marked on the map. Clearly these were "unofficial" tracks, some of them perhaps made by the deer and badgers that inhabited the area, and it was very hard to distinguish them from the "official" path that we were meant to be taking.

I had been told to allow the students to make their own mistakes, and only step in if it got hopeless. Sometimes we would stop at a fork and an argument would break out within the group as to whether or not it was the path they had planned. There were a lot of fruitless wanderings which resulted in us retracing our steps, and added many minutes, in fact probably a couple of hours, to our journey. The students began to get disheartened, and I noticed that as they lost confidence in their route and became discouraged, they appeared to feel the weight of their backpacks much more than they had when they were striding ahead with assurance. They were more inclined to complain and they lost patience with each other. Frankly I was of no help at all to them, other than to keep their spirits up (at one point I had them marching along to rousing choruses of "Lloyd George knew my father" and "Always look on the bright side of life"). But maps are a mystery to me, you might as well have handed me the periodic table, it was equally obscure.

Then I remembered something. As a teenager I had done a lot of sailing on the North Sea. Often, the landmarks ashore and the lights of the buoys and beacons were enough to steer a course by. But when the fog descended, all these visual markers disappeared, and the only hope of arriving safely at the desired harbour was to plot the course on the chart and set the compass to the right reading to take us there. Then no matter how disorientated we felt, even if we seemed to be going round in circles or back the way we had come, I learned that the compass was a far more reliable guide than my feelings. I learned to respect the compass and put my faith in it. It never lied and we always ended up at our planned destination.

Once I remembered this, the D of E walk became a whole lot easier. Every time we came to a fork and the students were not sure which path they should take, I got them to check the map and see which direction the path should be taking them. Then I made them take out the compass and see if the path they were contemplating did in fact go in that direction. They soon got the hang of this and progress became more rapid. The one thing they learned was what I had discovered on those sailing trips many years before – the compass never lies. You can trust it.

I am currently facing a fork in the path of my life, and I've been wondering which way to go. Three years ago I found myself facing the hardest decision of my life, one over which I had agonised long and hard. What I began to discover then was that the peace of God was like the compass for my life. The right decision is always the one that has God's signature peace on it. In Colossians 3 verse 15, it says, "Let the peace of Christ rule in your hearts." Or, as the Amplified Version renders it more fully, "And let the peace (soul harmony which comes) from Christ rule (act as umpire continually) in your hearts [deciding and settling with finality all questions that arise in your minds, in that peaceful state] to which as [members of Christ's] one body you were also called [to live]."

Two options lie before me. One is logical and sensible. It's what any level-headed friend would advise me to do. The other is risky, insecure and counter-intuitive. And strange to say, it's this latter one which fills my heart with the peace of Christ when I contemplate it. I am left in no doubt that God is calling me to an uncertain path, one which involves a leap of faith. The other one ought to offer more security and more peace of mind; and yet God's peace is absent the moment I begin to step foot on it. But I have learned to trust the compass.

I have had a very disorientating few months – another lifequake. It has left me hardly knowing which way is up. Neither of the available paths looks quite like the map I thought I had, and it's hard to be sure if I'm going on or back, or simply round in circles. I am going to trust the compass. As soon as I say to God, I am going to trust You, to trust Your provision for me, Your guiding, Your removal of all the obstacles that seem to bestrew this path, and I am going to walk this way, I sense God's approval , the joy and comfort of the Holy Spirit and the signature peace of God. The compass is pointing to true north, and although the way looks completely obscure and I certainly can't see where the path leads, or even where it emerges from under the dark trees into open land and broad daylight, I know that the compass never lies, and I'm going to trust it.

38. Progressing towards uncertainty and doubt

I'm taking a risk here, a risk of being misunderstood and labelled either a backslider or a heretic, so let me start by defining what I mean by certain key terms.

Belief is a mental assent to a proposition or set of propositions.

Faith is an act of total trust – it goes beyond mental assent to staking your all on something.

Unbelief is the absence of both belief and faith, and is an act of the will according to Hebrews 3.12 ("See to it, my brothers, that no evil, unbelieving heart is found in any of you.")

Doubt is a process of questioning your set of beliefs, and of being prepared to relinquish any not found to ring true.

I grew up with certainties. My parents had, quite literally, staked their all on what they knew to be true, and had given up a secure and well paid job to devote their lives to spreading the Gospel. And before I go any further I want to make it clear I don't have an ounce of criticism for them; they were faithfully following God on their journey, as I am following Him on mine. And so the faith I inherited was hedged around with certainties, and I believed them. I knew what you had to do to be guaranteed heaven. I knew who was in and who was out. I knew what God was like and what you had to do to please Him. I knew whom He was displeased with (very often me, actually). I knew exactly which box God fitted into, and if I heard something about God that I couldn't find in the Bible, I could safely dismiss it as error. I knew where God was to be found, and that to look for Him anywhere else was a dangerous occupation that could lead to demonic deception.

I also knew it was my duty to "witness", and so I went round proclaiming these certainties to everyone I knew and praying for those who rejected them. This made me a pain in the butt, a smug, superior, holier-than-thou know-it-all.

Since then, a lot has happened to change me. I discovered that you can pray all the right prayers but your child still winds up with multiple disabilities. You can do all the right things, pray, fast and agonise and still end up divorced. You can meet with callous accusations of inadequate faith from fellow-Christians but a Bah'ai friend totally demonstrates the accepting, welcoming heart of God to you. You can do a Religious Studies degree and find whole chunks in the Qur'an and the Guru Granth Sahib that you can say a hearty Amen to. You can try to keep God in that box He was in when you were growing up but He keeps breaking out all over the place.

I discovered that doubt, far from being a sin, was an authentic way to evaluate your beliefs and end up with truths you can really put your faith in. I discovered that certainty about God simply means you have made Him in your own image and stopped being open to some startling revelation from Him. I discovered that many people who were seeking God in places I had once thought dangerous were actually on a journey, catching glimpses of Him without always recognising Whom they were seeing. Some might never come to recognise Him but for many, loving a God whom they encountered outside Christendom might be the first step on a path that would lead them to Jesus.

I discovered that some of those certainties were absolutely valid and survived the scrutiny process intact. I absolutely affirm that Jesus is the Incarnation of God, that His name is above every other name in the universe and that one day He will return in glory and every human knee will bow and every tongue confess that He is Lord, to the glory of God the Father. I'm no longer sure that if you don't understand this you are automatically "out".

In many ways it has become more uncomfortable to try to hold on to old certainties than to live with uncertainty. Some scriptures which can seem very legalistic become so much more expansive when the filter through which you're looking at them is love rather than duty or expectations. Three years ago I lost my home, my husband, my ability to do my job – and the one unchanging, solid, dependable thing in all of this was Jesus. Now I feel as if even the Jesus I thought I knew doesn't exist and I must begin all over again getting to know Him as He really is. It's totally disorientating. Sometimes I feel as if I've lost my bearings in life – and yet it's also good because it's where He wants me. Above all, I'm finding out that His love and mercy and forgiveness have heights, breadths and depths that I have never dreamed of. How can I not accept myself, just the way I am, when He is apparently never unaccepting of me, no matter what I do? How can I hold on to old resentments and unforgiveness when He loves the other person no matter how much they have hurt me?

I remember one of the lasts visits of Roy Hicks Jr to our church, shortly before his untimely death. He talked about James and John demanding to sit either side of Jesus in His kingdom. Jesus asked if they could drink the cup He was about to drink, and be baptised with the baptism He was about to undergo, and with great bravado they assured Him they could. He didn't slap them down and say, "Oh no you can't!" He actually agreed that they would do those very things, but even so, it wasn't for Him to grant their request. And Roy Hicks pointed out that they didn't take umbrage or go off in a huff, because they had been around Jesus long enough to know that even when you've fulfilled all the conditions to get what you want and you don't get it, Jesus is still worth following.

I have a Jesus who didn't intervene to stop me being abducted as a child, who didn't send guardian angels to prevent my daughter suffering massive brain damage, who didn't save my marriage, even when I fasted, prayed, forgave over and over, and, despite my mistakes and imperfections, obeyed every single instruction I was aware of Him giving me. I don't have a Jesus I can believe in the way I used to do. But I have a Jesus I can put my faith in, a Jesus whose plans for redeeming and making use of my life experiences go way beyond my wildest imaginings. I have a Jesus who doesn't say, "Come unto Me in the right way with the correct formula and a sufficiently sincere degree of repentance and I will start work on cleaning you up and making you acceptable." I have a Jesus who says, "Stay right where you are, I'm on my way to rescue you, and the amount of love I'm about to shower on you will blow all your circuits." I have a Jesus who sometimes patiently watches me fulfil all the conditions to get what I'm asking for and then does nothing to ensure that I get it. And in the process I learn that it's not all about me, it's all about Him, and that in overturning a lot of my beliefs, I'm left with a Jesus I can put my faith in; a Jesus who won't stay in my neat boxes, who does things I could never have predicted, who includes people my pride would once have kept outside the door, and whose very unpredictability fills my life with a lot of joy and fun that was absent from all my former certainties and beliefs.